From Heidi Wenk Sormaz: To Nik

From Bruce Tulgan: To all of the people who have suffered as a result of poorly managed stress in the workplace.

Table of Contents

— v —

Acknowledgments

FIRST AND FOREMOST, we must thank the many thousands of incredible people who, over the years, have shared with RainmakerThinking the lessons of their own experiences in the workplace. We are also grateful to all the business leaders and managers who have expressed so much confidence in RainmakerThinking and our work; thank you for giving us the opportunity to learn from the real management issues you deal with and solve on a daily basis. And to the tens of thousands who have attended our seminars, thanks for listening, for laughing, for sharing the wisdom of your experience, for pushing us with the really tough questions, for all of your kindness, and for continually teaching us.

Second, Heidi wishes to acknowledge Nikola Sormaz for his support and Steven Bennett for his guidance.

Many thanks as well to our publisher, Bob Carkhuff, and his team at HRD Press, especially Mary George for her superb editing and book-design work. And thanks to all our colleagues, present and past, at RainmakerThinking.

Finally, for our families and our friends, we reserve our deepest and utmost gratitude.

Introduction

EVERYONE IN TODAY'S WORKPLACE is under pressure. We are living in an era of uncertainty, with wildly fluctuating markets and fiercely competitive business conditions. Organizations are determined to get more and better work out of fewer people, and most employees are routinely told they must work smarter, faster, better, longer, and harder. It is no wonder that study after study shows that managing stress is a growing challenge.

In general, we tend to think of stress as something negative; but in fact, it does have tangible benefits. Stress generates action. It creates a physiological boost that gives you increased energy and clarity with which to perform well. If channeled correctly, stress can enhance your performance and the performance of those you manage. Of course, if channeled incorrectly, stress can be overwhelming and performance will rapidly decline.

In today's complex world, most of us are susceptible to feeling and manifesting stress, at least sometimes, in all the different areas of our lives. The workplace in particular holds many potential stressors, so many that we are all in constant danger of "stressing out." The critical task for you as a manager, then, is to gain a better understanding of stress in the workplace, in your organization, and in teams and individuals. We encourage you to consider best practices for reducing stress, alleviating the effects of stress, and intervening to help "stressed-out" employees. However, there are limits to what a manager can do to help employees manage stress. Ultimately, to perform well under pressure, employees must develop stress management skills.

The good news is that, with training, all individuals can learn how to work well under pressure for optimal performance. The ability to perform well under pressure comes down to two skills:

1. Perceiving a situation in an optimal way (optimal perception)
2. Using the physiological boost associated with stress to one's advantage (optimal energy management)

Unfortunately, most individuals must work at developing these skills. That is the principle focus of this pocket guide.

Overview of the Pocket Guide

The explanations, analysis, and best practices in this pocket guide come directly from two sources: ongoing workplace research conducted by RainmakerThinking since the mid 1990s, and academic research conducted by Dr. Sormaz in her early career at Yale University as well as her independent research. Here is a brief outline of the material covered:

Part One: Managing Stress in the Workplace

✦ **Chapter 1. Stress in the Workplace.** Here we provide an overview of stress in general and workplace stress in particular. We look at the common causes of stress, the costs of poorly managed stress, and the potential benefits of well-managed stress.

✦ **Chapter 2. Managing Stress in Your Work Group or Organization.** This chapter presents organizational best practices for stress management.

✦ **Chapter 3. Managing the "Stressed-Out" Employee.** Here we offer advice for dealing with employees suffering from stress, including signs and symptoms to look for and steps for productively discussing the problem with the employee.

Part Two: Performance Under Pressure

✦ **Chapter 4. Clarify Your Relationship With Stress and Its Causes.** This chapter provides a self-assessment and other tools and suggestions to help the individual get started on developing effective stress management skills and habits.

✦ **Chapter 5. Optimal Energy Management: Stop and Breathe.** Here we introduce *Stop, Breathe, Rewrite, and Take Action (SBRT),* an effective four-step process for stress management. This chapter details the first two steps, Stop and Breathe, designed to promote optimal energy management.

+ **Chapter 6. Optimal Perception: Rewrite.** Our focus here is the third step of the SBRT process, Rewrite. This step promotes optimal perception, and is outlined with appropriate techniques and interventions.

+ **Chapter 7. Optimal Performance: Take Action.** This chapter details the fourth and final step of the SBRT process, Take Action. Whereas the first three steps allow you to decide what action is appropriate, this step involves how to take action to deal with a pressure situation.

+ **Chapter 8. Making SBRT a Habit.** The point of this chapter is to help you stop the habit of mismanaged pressure and replace it with the SBRT technique.

Finally, Chapters 9 through 13 focus on applying the SBRT technique to common stressful situations. They cover, respectively, five basic forms of pressure: time pressure, anger pressure, people pressure, fatigue pressure, and evaluation pressure.

Throughout this book, we've included:

- Clear and simple explanations
- Concrete action steps
- Room for brainstorming

- Exercises for applying the ideas and action steps to the stress management issues you are facing (or may face) in your own workplace

It is our great hope that this material will help you better understand the nature of stress, particularly stress in the workplace, as well as equip you with concrete best practices and tools for better managing stress in yourself and others.

If the ideas and strategies in these pages help you improve your working life and add to your success, then we have succeeded with this pocket guide. Please let us know—we'd love to hear from you. Contact us at www.rainmakerthinking.com.

Part One

Managing Stress in the Workplace

CHAPTER I

Stress in the Workplace

JOE WAS EXHAUSTED when he got out of bed this morning. Once again, he had not slept well—lately, a common problem for him. He was worried about work. There were not only several new tasks and responsi- bilities he had to juggle, but also a pressing deadline he was working hard to meet and very well might miss. Joe simply didn't feel like he could handle all the work on his plate.

Now Joe was running late. He couldn't stop thinking about his ill sister, to whom he hadn't spoken in days. It was impossible to find a good time to call. "No time, no time, no time," Joe said to himself, realizing there was no time for his morning exercise, either, or even time to shave. At least he could brush his teeth in the shower.

After quickly dressing, Joe pulled on his coat and launched at the kitchen cabinets for some semblance of breakfast. The cabinet doors seemed to fight against him, not opening fast enough. Then the items on the shelves decided to be difficult, getting in his way. "All I want is something to eat! Grrrr . . ." *Joe growled at them. As he shoved aside some soup cans, one caught on his coat sleeve. Out the cans tumbled as he pulled his arm away. Joe wanted to scream but just growled again—and grabbed a candy bar from the refrigerator.*

Munching on his "nutritious" breakfast, Joe finally made it to his car. He had to check every pocket, it seemed, before he got his hands on his keys; then he fumbled trying to open the car door. Finally, he started the car and pulled out of the driveway. He raced off—only to hit every single traffic light, or so it seemed, on his way to work.

By the time Joe found a parking space and made it into work, he was genuinely late. He checked his in-box for the report he was expecting from his assistant Frank. "Nothing," he said to himself. "How am I supposed to get anything done when people are always letting me down?" Joe then noticed his voicemail light blinking. He listened to the message, which was from his boss, Mary. "The sooner the better, Joe," she said about the project he was supposed to be finishing.

Joe sat down at his desk and tried to work, but his thoughts were swimming. He couldn't concentrate. Still, he turned on his computer and pulled open his drawer so he could start reading through a file while his computer was booting up. He wasn't sure whether to scream or to cry. But something had to give, and soon.

What Is Stress?

We've all dealt with "stressed-out" people in our personal lives and probably in our working lives. And we all know how it feels to be under pressure and feel stress. But what exactly is stress?

Stress is a fundamental human reaction, with mental, emotional, and physiological dimensions. Like other primal reactions, it is rooted in our instinct for self-preservation. Virtually all our bodily systems undergo modification in response to "stressors," the term experts use to describe the causes of stress.

Stressors are perceived dangers to one's well-being. They may be external or internal; direct or indirect; physical or psychological; acute or chronic. Certain factors may increase one's susceptibility to stressors, including physiological conditions, inherited characteristics, early childhood experiences, the duration of and type of stressors, youth or advanced age, and circumstantial vulnerability.

For examples of stressors, we might point to major life crises, such as deaths and career pitfalls, and long-term problems such as abusive relationships. Common acute stressors include discomfort, excessive temperatures, noise, hunger, too little (or too much) exercise, infections, disapproval, limited time, loneliness, exploitation, frustration, conflict, manipulation, betrayal, and humiliation.

In response to acute stressors, the brain releases hormones (including the steroid hormone cortisol) and neurotransmitters (including adrenaline), and the heart, lungs, and circulatory systems increase performance. All these physiological responses marshal the resources of the body.

Stress also affects our perceptions, thought processes, communication, and behavior, helping us respond to stressors more effectively by intensifying our mental focus. This explains why stress can be an important asset for raising levels of performance during critical events and crises and in dangerous situations.

Although stress can boost performance, when it is not managed properly, the physical and psychological responses can become extreme. These responses may continue to affect us after the critical event has ended, thus diminishing our physical resources and our mental capacity. Instead of being strengthened by stress, we are weakened. Instead of gaining mental clarity, we suffer thought distortions and memory loss and have problems concentrating, communicating, and taking effective action. And when poorly managed stress becomes chronic, it can cause great damage to the body and mind.

The important thing to remember is that stress, per se, is neither negative nor positive. Stressors are inevitable and are important signals to our body and mind about our environment and circumstances. It is our individual interpretation of the stressors and our ability to respond effectively to them that determines whether stress will have positive or negative consequences.

Stress in the Workplace

Most of us deal with stressors on a regular basis in every area of our lives. Of those areas, work tends to present us with a particularly high frequency of stress. Depending upon the study you happen to read, you will find varying percentages of employees who report that they find their jobs stressful.

Among the many stressors mentioned by employees, these are the most common:

- The way my boss/supervisor treats me
- Lack of job security
- Company policies
- Coworkers who don't do their fair share
- Unclear expectations
- Poor communication
- Not enough control over assignments
- Inadequate pay or benefits
- Urgent deadlines
- Too much work
- Long hours
- Uncomfortable physical conditions
- Relationship conflicts
- Coworkers making careless mistakes
- Dealing with rude customers

- Lack of cooperation
- How the company treats coworkers
- How the company treats me

Job-related stress may result from any of these acute stressors; however, in the workplace, there are many systemic factors that also put employees at risk of chronic stress. These systemic factors include:

- Relationships that are interdependent, competitive, hierarchical, overexposed, and compulsory

- Financial and personal risk associated with pursuing a goal, facing a crisis, or seizing an opportunity

- Local effects of the global economy

- Downsizing and uncertainty about the fate of markets

Let us now review both the costs and the potential benefits of stress in the workplace.

The Costs of Stress in the Workplace

Stress becomes costly when people respond poorly to stressors. What happens? The individual's physiological response to the stressor, or threatening event, remains at a high level after the stressor has been removed or eliminated. This is commonly caused by overreaction to the actual event, with the response spiraling out of control. The physiological boost keeps climbing, far beyond what is necessary to deal with the situation.

What is the result of the poor response? Think of the stressed-out employee who flies off the handle, or the one who is always frantically multitasking to deal with an overwhelming workload, or the one who finally burns out and simply quits. Such poorly managed stress may result in violence, verbal outbursts, disruptive interactions, and hurt feelings, affecting everyone exposed to it. The costs of these results are obvious. Less obvious are the costs of stress that include damage to the individual, ranging from diminished career prospects to diminished health; damage to the work group, ranging from lost work time to lost innovation; and damage to the organization, ranging from increased absenteeism to increased turnover.

While it is difficult to calculate the monetary value of direct and indirect costs to individuals and organizations, we can enumerate some of the leading costly impacts of poorly managed stress.

Impact on the Person Experiencing Stress

For the individual, poorly managed stress causes strong emotional and physical responses resulting in impaired cognitive and physical functioning. Poorly managed stress, then, can damage a person's career, and if the stress is chronic, long-term health problems can result.

Here are the specifics:

Immediate Physical Components of Acute Stress

- Hypothalamic-pituitary-adrenal system is activated.
- Steroid hormones (glucocorticoids) are released.
- Heartbeat, respiratory rate, circulation, metabolism, immune systems increase.
- Blood pressure rises.
- Muscles in chest, back, and arms may tense up.
- Body may sweat, flush, or pale; feel clammy.

Immediate Psychological Components of Acute Stress

- Thought distortions
- Increased impulsiveness
- Increased feelings of fear
- Increased feelings of impatience
- Increased feelings of distress
- Diminished ability to reason
- Diminished ability to handle complex social or intellectual tasks

Long-Term Psychological Problems Related to Chronic Stress

- Diminished feelings of pleasure and accomplishment
- Diminished sense of well-being
- Depression
- Anxiety

In addition, stress can even cause suicide.

Long-Term Health Problems Related to Chronic Stress

- Heart disease
- Hypertension
- Stroke
- Susceptibility to infections
- Immune disorders
- Gastrointestinal disorders
- Headaches
- Respiratory disorders
- Skin disorders
- Arthritis
- Disabilities of the nervous system
- Eating disorders
- Sleep disorders
- Memory, concentration, and learning disorders
- Workplace injuries

Potential Career-Related Problems Resulting From Acute and Chronic Stress

- Inefficient use of time
- Difficulty concentrating
- Diminished speed and quality of work
- Trouble integrating new information
- Bad decision-making
- Increased relationship conflict
- Diminished motivation

Impact on the Work Group and Organization

Stress can also be very costly to the work group and organization. The first casualties are usually those who work closely with the problem individuals. The work group and organization then suffer from the radiating impact of the poorly managed stress.

When individuals experience a stressful relationship conflict with a more powerful person, they tend to take out their tension on someone entirely unrelated to the episode, usually someone less powerful. That's how stress from one boss can cascade down the ranks. Another corollary effect occurs when those who suffer from the cascading effects of stress respond with covert action (for example, by failing to cooperate or to communicate, or by undermining the other person's goals). According to one study, those suffering from cascading stress often respond with worry and preoccupation; this leads to avoidance behavior that diminishes their work performance, including lost effort and lost work time.

The following summarizes the dangers.

Consequences of Poorly Managed Stress to the Work Group and Organization

- Increased relationship conflict
- Lost work time
- Diminished commitment
- Diminished effort

- Diminished information-sharing
- Diminished risk-taking
- Diminished collaboration
- Delayed decision-making
- Lack of good data for decision making
- Diminished productivity
- Diminished work quality
- Diminished innovation
- Increased absenteeism
- Increased turnover
- Sabotage
- Litigation
- Verbal aggression
- Physical aggression
- Increased disability claims
- Increased health-care costs

Perhaps the greatest damage to a work group or an organization occurs when individuals perceive that stressful conditions are tolerated and even perpetuated by leaders and managers. When this happens, people feel let down by their leaders and begin to view the organizational culture as damaging and the organization as unsupportive of employees.

The Potential Benefits of Stress in the Workplace

For stress to be beneficial, it must be managed well, in an adaptive manner. This involves recognizing a stressor, perceiving it optimally, and responding appropriately (as described in Chapters 5 through 7). Such adaptive response gives you the extra energy and motivation you need to perform optimally while in the threatening situation and allows your physiology to return to a normal level once the stressful situation is over. In short, you use the brief increase in nervous-system activity as extra energy for dealing effectively with the situation at hand and then relax, allowing the system to return to baseline.

This adaptive response to stress eliminates the long-term psychological and health problems associated with chronic stress. In addition, the adaptive response also eliminates the career-related problems that may result from acute and chronic stress.

The physical changes in response to stressors can be very powerful in helping us to adapt to meet threatening conditions.

- For individuals, the stress response can provide the resources they need to increase performance levels at critical moments.

- For the work group, acute stress may indicate that members share a common interest in the group's success, care about that success, and will pull together in a common effort to achieve a common goal.

Thus stress may contribute to better outcomes as long as it is well managed and focused on the work itself—

allocation of resources, goal setting, task planning, and task execution.

When stress is *focused on the work itself,* it can be highly valuable. Such stress can do a number of things:

1. Act as a channel for energy that fuels intensive work and long hours

2. Lead someone to persist in pursuit of difficult goals against the odds

3. Act as a channel for creativity and innovation

4. Lead to debates over competing points of view, resulting in better decisions

5. Lead to healthy competition, which drives productivity and quality

6. Indicate important data about policies, practices, relationships, behavior, and conditions

7. Lead to improvements in the above when the data is handled properly

Complete the following worksheet to see whether you are tapping into the benefits of stress in the workplace. Keep in mind that how you interpret stressors and respond to them is the key to whether stress will have positive or negative consequences; whether acute stress will give you strength or weaken you; and whether the stress will dissipate appropriately or become chronic.

✦ WORKSHEET
Tapping the Benefits of Stress in the Workplace

Directions: Consider the following questions.

1. Have you ever had occasion to become stressed about work itself—the allocation of resources, goal setting, task planning, and/or task execution? If so, do you remember the details? When was this? What was at stake? Why were you stressed? What happened as a result of your stress?

2. Have you ever used the energy of stress to fuel intensive work and long hours? If so, how did you do that?

➡

Worksheet Continued

3. Has stress ever led you to persist against the odds in pursuit of difficult goals? If so, how did it do that?

4. Have you ever channeled stress into creativity and innovation? If so, how did you do that?

5. Has stress ever led you to engage in a debate over competing points of view, resulting in better decisions? If so, how did it do that?

6. Has stress ever led you into healthy competition? If so, with whom? How did it play out?

7. Has stress ever motivated you to face a strong competitor? If so, how did it motivate you? How did the situation turn out?

8. Has stress ever motivated you to confront wrongdoers? If so, how did it motivate you? How did the situation turn out?

9. Has stress ever helped you draw attention to injustice? If so, how did it help you? How did the situation turn out?

Worksheet Continued

10. Has stress ever pointed to important data about policies, practices, relationships, behavior, and conditions? If so, what happened in response to that data? Did it lead to improvements? How do you feel about it now?

11. Have you ever had an experience where work-focused stress degenerated into interpersonal stress? If so, why did that happen? Did the stress lead to fruitful discussion, resolution, and action? Did it lead to improving a strained relationship? Why or why not?

• *Worksheet Concluded*

The Importance of Stress Management

As we have seen in this chapter, stress is common to us all but can be positive or negative depending upon how well we manage it. In some cases, stressors may be eliminated or reduced; however, other stressors will take their place—they are inevitable.

The workplace in particular is likely to produce systemic and acute stressors. In response, individuals will experience the physiological, emotional, and psychological reactions they are programmed by nature to experience. Indeed, these reactions allow us to achieve increased levels of performance during critical times. However, when we fail to perceive stressors optimally, and our physical and psychological responses become exaggerated, our physical resources and mental capacity can be severely diminished.

Over time, poor stress management can lead to chronic stress, which carries significant risks to the individual's well-being and career. Poorly managed stress can also cause great damage to the work group and organization.

The key to tapping the benefits and minimizing the costs of stress in the workplace is effective stress management. There are three leading strategies for stress management:

1. Reducing stressors
2. Providing support services to those who are subject to significant stressors
3. Training individuals to better manage their stress

All three approaches have benefits. The first and second will be discussed in the next two chapters, which deal with the manager's role in managing stress in the work group or organization and managing the individual employee under stress. However, the most efficacious approach to stress management comes through improved individual coping-skills. Thus we have dedicated Part Two of this pocket guide to the third approach, training individuals in stress management techniques.

CHAPTER 2

Managing Stress in Your Work Group or Organization

IF YOU ARE IN A POSITION of organizational or team leadership, then you should continually assess the workplace to identify its strengths and weaknesses. This includes the tracking of stress. We've already discussed the tremendous costs that a team or company can incur if stress is poorly managed. Yet we know that systemic and acute factors make workplace stress unavoidable.

Most experts would agree that stressors vary in quantity and quality depending upon the work group and organization. The workplace in certain industries—such as health care and public safety—is apt to generate stress because of the urgent, critical nature of the work. In a 24/7/365 environment with life and death stakes, stressors are omnipresent. But as most leaders and managers will tell you, other factors can play a role in generating stress. Common factors and work examples include:

- Emotional content—counseling, teaching, and the arts
- Physical difficulty—mining, loading, and delivery

- High degree of repetition—data entry, telemarketing, and manufacturing

Indeed, there are so many potentially stress-inducing factors in so many different lines of work, it is important to caution leaders and managers to stay away from the "our industry is different" pitfall.

Three-Step Approach to Managing a Stressful Workplace

Often leaders and managers resign themselves to operating in a stressful workplace; they become convinced that stress is entirely unavoidable in their particular industry, a particular role, particular tasks and responsibilities, and particular work environments. Do not resign yourself to leading or managing a stressful environment. Take a systematic approach:

1. Assess your work group or organization.
2. Consider organizational best practices for stress management.
3. Provide support services to alleviate the negative effects of stress.

I. Assess Your Work Group or Organization

The following assessment will help you gauge the level of stress in your work group or organization. If you wish, complete the assessment twice, once for your work group and once for your organization.

✦ ASSESSMENT
Stress in Your Work Group or Organization

Directions: Answer the questions below to gauge the state of stress in your work group or organization.

1. Does your work group or organization exhibit any of the following symptoms of an unhealthy degree of stress? Check off those you have noticed.

   ❑ Absenteeism
   ❑ Increased workers-compensation claims
   ❑ Litigation
   ❑ Grievances
   ❑ Accidents
   ❑ Errors of judgment or action
   ❑ Conflict and interpersonal problems
   ❑ Violence
   ❑ Customer-service problems
   ❑ Vendor-management problems
   ❑ Resistance to management initiatives
   ❑ Resistance to management instructions
   ❑ Resistance to change
   ❑ Missed deadlines
   ❑ Diminished productivity
   ❑ Diminished quality
   ❑ Sabotage

   Note that although the above may indicate unhealthy stress levels, they may also derive from other sources. If you marked several, then your work group or organization has a problem, and it might be unhealthy stress.

2. What are some causes of stress in your particular work environment? Are there certain individuals who contribute

   ➡

unduly to the stress? Certain relationship issues? Specific projects? Specific tasks and responsibilities? Workload? Working conditions? Something about the work space? Something about the scheduling of the work? Tight deadlines? Something else?

3. Are some people in your workplace under more stress than others? If so, who? Why are they under more stress?

4. Do people in your workplace complain that they have no control over their work? If so, who? How often? What happens?

Assessment Continued

5. Do some people in your workplace exhibit aggression or engage in other inappropriate behavior? If so, who? How often? What happens?

6. Do some people in your workplace "burn out"? If so, who? How often? What happens?

7. Do some people in your workplace work excessive hours? If so, who? How often? What happens?

8. Do some people in your workplace complain of exhaustion? If so, who? How often? What happens?

9. Do some people in your workplace report relationship troubles at home? If so, who? How often? What happens?

10. Do some people in your workplace refuse to communicate with or refuse to work with other individuals, teams, departments, vendors, or customers? If so, who? How often? What happens?

Considering your responses above, rate the stress level of your work group or organization on a scale of 1 (low stress) to 10 (high stress).

Rating:

• *Assessment Concluded*

Perhaps you now have a better understanding of the role that stress is playing in your work group or organization. Keep in mind that our assessment is only a small step—a reality check—toward identifying a potential problem. It may be necessary to engage the work group or sample respondents from the organization in a more thorough investigation. The methods available to you will depend upon the size of the group or organization and your available resources; also, the most appropriate method may depend upon your initial assessment of the gravity of the issues facing the group or organization. You might consider a formal assessment by a professional team—either internal or external to your organization. Or you may wish to organize discussions in your group or organization to really get a handle on the issue.

Whatever method of investigation you use, if you suspect that stress is a problem in your work group or organization, you should clarify the nature of the problem and prepare to take steps to address it.

2. Consider Organizational Best Practices for Stress Management

The most direct action a manager can take to reduce unhealthy stress is to identify and remove unnecessary stressors from the workplace. In Chapter 1, we provided a list of common workplace stressors, which ranged from time schedules to physical conditions to interpersonal relationships. In general, good management

practices will likely reduce unhealthy stress; such practices include improving employee autonomy, training,
working conditions, schedules, career development,
support systems, communication, relationships with
supervisors, and reward opportunities. However, it is
not enough to say that a well-run organization with good
managers is unlikely to have pervasive problems with
stress. Therefore, it is important to consider the following stress-management best practices:

1. Promote employee decision-making.

2. Require leaders and managers to model
   appropriate behavior.

3. Do not select or promote people who fail to
   manage their stress.

4. Provide resources for stress management.

5. Form a committee to maintain focus on the
   issue.

I. Promote Employee Decision-Making.

Most individuals want to have input on matters that affect them, whether the effect is direct or indirect. They
are far less likely to experience unhealthy stress when
they have a reasonable degree of control over their work
schedules, workspace, tasks, responsibilities, learning
opportunities, relationships, and compensation. Indeed,
the more control someone has over these factors, the
more apt that person is to perform demanding work
without experiencing unhealthy stress.

2. Require Leaders and Managers to Model Appropriate Behavior.

Stress tends to move downward through hierarchies. Since employees scrutinize their leaders' behavior for signs of appropriate conduct, leaders should model stress management. Their behavior should allow the appropriate expression of stress and not permit it to spiral out of control. Also, their authority gives them the responsibility to provide support, coaching, and empowerment.

3. Do Not Select or Promote People Who Fail to Manage Their Stress.

When selecting individuals for open positions or for promotions, be sure to evaluate their skills and track record on stress management. Often organizations hire and promote people on the sole basis of financial or technical performance. Although such performance is certainly valuable, the value is outweighed by the damage inflicted on individuals, teams, and organizations when these people—especially those in positions of authority—express their stress aggressively and repeatedly. Selection criteria and all performance evaluations should give considerable weight to individual stress management, interpersonal skills, and the ability to build work-group morale.

4. Provide Resources for Stress Management.

In the workplace, it is important to build general awareness of job stress, to secure management involvement and support, and to secure employee involvement. Provide individuals with self-study materials and training programs that will help them learn how to manage their own stress. In addition, provide managers with training in stress management, conflict resolution, negotiation, and coaching. We equip you with a framework for stress-management training in Part Two of this pocket guide.

5. Form a Committee to Maintain Focus on the Issue.

Some leaders and managers may wish to consider the formation of an occupational stress committee to maintain focus on the issue in their workplace. Such a committee may be charged with such tasks as monitoring symptoms of unhealthy stress, identifying unnecessary stressors and ways to reduce them, providing support services to alleviate the effects of stress, and sponsoring stress management training. If you form such a committee, make sure it is representative of the employee population, includes managers as well, and has a clear charge of responsibility and authority.

3. Provide Support Services to Alleviate the Negative Effects of Stress

This is a simple but important step for reducing stress and/or alleviating its effects in a work group or an organization. There are many different types of services, which are more or less appropriate depending on the work situation at hand. Also, different services are more or less feasible for different employers. Services offered by various organizations include athletic facilities and fitness programs, family care (elder and child care), and concierge services such as personal shopping or dry-cleaning. A more extensive list of support services can be found in the Appendix.

The Importance of Managing Stress in Your Work Group or Organization

As we have seen in this chapter, if you are in a leadership position, you must be aware of the potential for unhealthy stress in your work group or organization and be prepared to take action to address it. Do not resign yourself to unhealthy stress levels in your workplace. Be sure to complete the assessment earlier in this chapter, but remember that it is just a reality check—a more extensive assessment, conducted by an internal or external professional team, may be needed.

Whatever your investigation method, if you suspect that stress is a problem, you should clarify the problem's nature and prepare to take steps to address it. The most direct action you can take is to identify and remove unnecessary stressors from the workplace. Good management practices will help reduce unhealthy stress, but you should also consider implementing the stress-management best practices we have outlined. Finally, depending upon your resources, you may wish to provide your employees with support services to alleviate some of the effects of unhealthy stress.

In closing, we want to emphasize that while systemic factors have a major impact on stress, stress is largely an individuated phenomenon and it is impossible for a company to predict and control all potential workplace stressors. It is thus important for individuals to learn stress management techniques—our focus in Part Two. First, though, we will address the steps you can take if you are managing a particular individual who seems to be suffering from unhealthy stress.

Managing the "Stressed-Out" Employee

IN THE WORKPLACE, you interact with a great many people—customers, vendors, peers, subordinates, and bosses. Any of them might have problems with stress, and those problems can be rooted in any of a wide range of causes. It is not always appropriate for you to engage the person on the matter. But there is one case where you must take responsibility: When an employee over whom you have direct supervisory authority is suffering the effects of poorly managed stress, you must take action to help.

What should you do? Dealing with an individual under stress is a highly personal matter and must be handled delicately. First you must assess the person. Everyone is different, and the most effective way to deal with any particular individual depends upon a host of factors. Is the person generally approachable or not? Aggressive or passive? Does the person tend to listen? Does he or she have a track record of responding well to feedback? Do you have some kind of rapport with the person? In what ways is the individual manifesting stress? To what degree is the individual manifesting stress? Do you know the cause? Can the cause be addressed easily?

Depending upon the nature and gravity of the situation, you may or may not be the one to provide the ultimate solution. But as the person's manager, it is your responsibility to intervene.

Three Steps for Managing an Employee Under Stress

To manage the stressed-out employee, take these three basic steps:

1. Recognize the signs and symptoms of stress in the employee.
2. Engage the employee in productive discussion.
3. Take action to help the employee.

I. Recognize the Signs and Symptoms of Stress

As we have seen, people under stress exhibit a broad range of physical, psychological, and behavioral signs and symptoms. Of course, diagnosis is the business of medical professionals, and unless you have the necessary training, you cannot make a medical diagnosis yourself. As a manager, though, you should be sufficiently aware of the signs and symptoms to know when stress may be a problem for an employee. A list of these is included on the worksheet provided later in this section.

The first thing to remember is that not all employees will exhibit the same signs and symptoms of stress. There are two primary types of people: stress-out and stress-in. Stress-out types tend experience intensely stressful feelings and over-express those feelings in visible behavior. For that reason, their stress is easier to identify. Stress-in types tend to under-express their stress; so their behavioral indications are less noticeable.

Second, as we noted earlier, individuals often suffer from the symptoms of stress for reasons entirely unrelated to stress; thus symptoms alone are not enough to diagnose stress. As a manager, you should look at symptoms in the larger context of what you know about the employee and his or her work situation. If you don't have sufficient information on your own, you may have to gather information in order to make a reasonable judgment about whether or not the employee is actually experiencing unhealthy stress.

It is important to determine whether or not the employee has been exposed to one or more acute stressors in the workplace or at home. If you are not a medical professional, the best you can do at this point is make a preliminary evaluation. The next step, engaging the employee in a productive discussion, will supply you with further information. You can then see if there is something you can do to help. Once again, keep in mind that stress can be a serious enough problem to warrant the help of a medical professional.

✦ WORKSHEET
Looking for the Signs and Symptoms of Stress

Directions: Answer the following questions, using the lists of signs and symptoms as a guide. Remember that these listed items may be caused by something other than stress.

1. In what ways and to what degree is the employee exhibiting stress?

SIGNS AND SYMPTOMS

Short-Term Physical	Short-Term Psychological
Stomach problems	Forgetfulness
Headaches	Frustration
Fatigue	Anger
Muscle aches and pains	Anxiety
Skin rashes	Irritability
Teeth grinding/Muscle tics	Sadness
Chronic mild illness	Depression

➡

Worksheet Continued

Short-Term Behavioral

Expressing powerlessness

Avoidance behavior

Withdrawing from socialization

Obsessing over insignificant
details

Lateness

Personality conflicts

Outbursts

Frequent Mistakes

Errors in judgment

Use of drugs, alcohol,
cigarettes

Over- or under-eating

Sleep disturbances

2. Has the employee recently been exposed to physical, psychological, or occupational stressors? If so, which ones?

STRESSORS

Physical

Chemical agents

Noise

Heat or cold

Hazards

Repetition

Heavy loads

Long hours

Uncomfortable work space

Psychological

Fear

Anger

Sadness

Insecurity or risk

Insult or humiliation

Urgency

Manipulation

Worksheet Continued

Occupational

Increased work goals	Relationship conflict
New tasks and responsibilities	Lack of input in decisions
Diminished tasks/responsibilities	Conflicting demands
Diminished autonomy	Failure
Diminished authority	Poor Communication

• *Worksheet Concluded*

2. Engage the Employee in a Productive Discussion

If you suspect an employee is suffering from unhealthy stress, engage him or her in a productive discussion. Schedule a meeting with the person to gather information, to talk about the problem you perceive, and to offer your assistance. Be strategic about the time and place of the meeting; you want to have a conversation free from distraction in a place that conveys concern and support for the person.

Give yourself time to prepare for the meeting. Question your assumptions and suspend judgment. Gather information and rehearse what you are going to say; also, decide what you are *not* going to say. Remember that your goal in the discussion is fourfold:

1. To listen carefully
2. To determine whether your initial assessment of the problem was accurate

3. To judge the gravity of the situation
4. To figure out whether there is anything you can do to help

Be prepared to help the employee, but realize that you must avoid the mistake of playing therapist.

Open the discussion with an explanation of why you asked for the meeting. Explain that you have noticed certain signs and symptoms and that you think they may be linked to the causes you have preliminarily identified. Then quickly shift to asking good open-ended questions such as:

- *How are you feeling lately?*
- *What's on your mind?*
- *How has [such and such] change affected you?*

Listen carefully and actively, but don't interrupt. Guide the discussion only when necessary and with neutral but probing questions such as *How?, Why?,* and *Can you be more specific?* Try to gather more data. Throughout, exhibit respect, sensitivity, open-mindedness, flexibility, and tolerance.

While you want to be focused on the individual during the meeting—making eye contact, nodding your head, showing concern, smiling if there is an appropriate moment—you also want to take notes. This signals that you are taking the matter seriously and that there will be a record of the conversation.

It may be necessary, at some point in the conversation, to provide constructive feedback on how the individual expressed his or her stress. If the person handled the situation well, you should offer positive feedback to reinforce the behavior. If the person expressed stress in an unacceptable or inappropriate way, you must address the matter directly. Explain your expectations for behavior in similar situations.

Once you have gained sufficient information from the discussion and given any needed feedback, seek a solution to the problem. You may have suggestions about support or assistance that you or someone else in the organization might provide. However, before making these suggestions, probe further to see if the individual has given thought to support or assistance that he or she would like to receive. Take this approach:

- First, explain that you may be unable to do everything the person wants or needs.
- Then ask, *What can I do to help you?*

Be sure the answers are specific; and again, listen carefully and take notes. If you need time to consider the person's requests, reconvene the meeting at a later date. If the person has no concrete requests, offer your own suggestions or ideas. The result of the discussion must be some kind of productive response to the stress. You must be prepared to take action to help the employee.

➤ **Steps for Engaging the Employee**

1. Schedule a meeting with the employee to gather information, to talk about the problem you perceive, and to offer your assistance.

2. Prepare for the meeting.

3. At the meeting, explain that you have noticed certain signs and symptoms and that you think they may be linked to the causes you have preliminarily identified.

4. Ask open-ended questions such as *How are you feeling lately? What's on your mind? How has [such and such] change affected you?*

5. Guide the discussion only when necessary, and use neutral but probing questions such as *How? Why? Can you be more specific?* Take notes.

6. Provide any necessary feedback.

7. Explain that you may be unable to do everything the person wants or needs; then ask, *What can I do to help you?* Take notes.

3. Take Action to Help the Employee

Before taking action, you must answer three questions:

- Is there a clear stressor?

- Is the stressor a necessary component of the job or workplace?

- If not a necessary component, can the stressor be removed?

> ➤ *Questions for Taking Action*

1. Is there a clear stressor? Is it a necessary component of the job or workplace? If not, can the stressor be removed?

2. Can you offer small adjustments in work conditions?

3. If the stressors cannot be removed, are there support services offered by your organization that may help alleviate the effects of stress?

4. If the stressors cannot be removed, are there resources or training available to help the employee develop stress management skills?

5. Is professional help necessary?

Sometimes a small adjustment in an employee's work conditions can have a huge impact. If you are in a position to make such an adjustment, you should attempt to do so. If, however, you cannot remove the stressor in question, you have three options:

- Refer the person to support services in your organization that may help alleviate the effects of stress; or

- Direct the person to appropriate resources or training to develop stress management skills; or

- Help the person realize that he or she is simply not a good fit with the job or workplace.

Finally, if you determine that the stress may be serious or may pose a risk to the employee or coworkers, you must refer the employee to professional help.

Part Two

Performance Under Pressure

CHAPTER 4

Clarify Your Relationship With Stress and Its Causes

THERE ARE LIMITS to what a manager can do to help employees manage stress in the workplace. Ultimately, to perform under pressure, employees must develop stress management skills. And to develop these skills, employees must first assess their current relationship with stress.

As we have seen, stress is a complex response that involves thinking (cognition) and feeling (emotion) as well as physiology. Stress can be caused by many different factors, and can be expressed in many different ways or repressed to various degrees. Work in particular is full of the type of pressures that will physically and psychologically make you or break you. Studies have shown that the ability to handle stressors like those encountered at work is actually more important than the handling of major life crises when it comes to maintaining physical and psychological well-being. In addition, environmental and lifestyle factors may contribute to a person's overall susceptibility to stress.

What is your own relationship with stress? Take a few minutes to become more aware of this relationship, and the factors that may contribute to it, by completing the following two self-assessments.

✦ SELF-ASSESSMENT I
Exploring Your Own Stress

Directions: Explore your relationship with stress by answering the questions below.

1. Do you think you are under a lot of stress? What makes you think so (either way)?

2. Has anyone ever told you that you're stressed out? If so, who? Under what circumstances? How many times have you heard that?

3. How often would you say that you feel the effects of stress?

➡

Assessment Continued

4. Do you lose your temper often? If so, under what circum-
    stances? How often?

5. Do you feel out of control? If so, under what circum-
    stances? How often?

6. Do you feel overburdened? Or overwhelmed? If so, under
    what circumstances? How often?

7. Do you sometimes become highly irritated over small
    inconveniences? If so, how often does this sort of thing
    happen? Why do you think it happens?

8. How do you behave when you feel stress?

9. Do you have trouble sleeping? If so, under what circumstances? How often?

10. Are you feeling troubling physical symptoms? If so, what are they? How often do you experience them?

11. Have you been having trouble in relationships at work or at home? If so, under what circumstances? How often?

• *Assessment Concluded*

✦ SELF-ASSESSMENT 2
Exploring Your Own Stressors

Directions: How much stress are you under at work, in your environment, and in your lifestyle? By completing all three parts of this assessment, you will be one small step closer to the answer.

1. Check off any event that has occurred in the last year. The more checkmarks you make, the more likely it is that you feel pressure at work on a daily basis.

   ❏ Too much work
   ❏ Too little work
   ❏ A change in job responsibilities
   ❏ An outstanding performance achievement
   ❏ Trouble with the boss
   ❏ A change in working hours
   ❏ A change in working conditions
   ❏ Working with new people
   ❏ Pressure to meet deadlines
   ❏ Requirement to perform beyond your ability
   ❏ Keeping up with new technology
   ❏ Constant change of policies or procedures
   ❏ Lack of clear job objectives
   ❏ No social support
   ❏ Given responsibility but not control
   ❏ Feelings of pressure from your boss
   ❏ Telephone interruptions
   ❏ Lack of promotion
   ❏ Boredom
   ❏ Work demands on private life

Assessment Continued

2. Now consider your environment and lifestyle. In the inventory below, list the events and things that make you feel stressed; then consider whether any of them can be avoided or if you can make helpful adjustments.

EVENT/THING	IS IT AVOIDABLE?	POSSIBLE ADJUSTMENTS

3. For another approach, look at your typical daily schedule and then fill in the details on the following Inventory chart. Be as thorough as you can about what you usually do during each time period: Where are you, with whom, doing what, and how? Then think about which aspects of your environment and lifestyle are most likely to cause stress. Can you think of any adjustments that might reduce stress?

TIME	TYPICAL SCHEDULE: Who, what, where, how?	SOMETIMES A CAUSE OF STRESS? (Yes/No)	POSSIBLE ADJUSTMENTS
AM			
12:00			
1:00			
2:00			
3:00			
4:00			
5:00			
6:00			
7:00			

ENVIRONMENTAL AND LIFESTYLE INVENTORY: TYPICAL DAY

ENVIRONMENTAL AND LIFESTYLE INVENTORY: TYPICAL DAY			
TIME	TYPICAL SCHEDULE: Who, what, where, how?	SOMETIMES A CAUSE OF STRESS? (Yes/No)	POSSIBLE ADJUSTMENTS
8:00			
9:00			
10:00			
11:00			
PM			
12:00			
1:00			
2:00			
3:00			

ENVIRONMENTAL AND LIFESTYLE INVENTORY: TYPICAL DAY			
TIME	TYPICAL SCHEDULE: Who, what, where, how?	SOMETIMES A CAUSE OF STRESS? (Yes/No)	POSSIBLE ADJUSTMENTS
4:00			
5:00			
6:00			
7:00			
8:00			
9:00			
10:00			
11:00			

•Assessment Concluded

Perhaps you are now one step closer to understanding your own stress. If you think that you are experiencing problems with chronic stress, you should consider the help of a psychotherapist. However, even with the assistance of a professional (or someone who knows you well and whom you deeply trust), ultimately it is you who must evaluate and address your stress. Many people never examine their lives in this way, but all of us need to do it.

CHAPTER 5

Optimal Energy Management: Stop and Breathe

NOW THAT YOU have reviewed your relationship with stress, you need to take charge of your responses to it. This involves developing a plan and a set of stress management skills so that you will be able to thrive under pressure. Chapters 5 through 7 present an effective process for doing just that. Its techniques reflect the principle that performing well under pressure requires optimal energy management and optimal perception.

The four steps of this process were first described by the Mind/Body Medical Institute of New England Deaconess Hospital and Harvard Medical School. We have expanded their approach based upon our own research and experience. We describe these steps as **Stop – Breathe – Rewrite – Take Action,** or **SBRT.**

- **Stop** refers to interrupting the rise of mental and physical symptoms.
- **Breathe** means engaging in deep breathing; this immediately counteracts the typical physiological response to pressure and keeps it under control.

- **Rewrite** is the process of noticing and challenging your thoughts.
- **Take Action** refers to the implementation of a problem-solving approach to respond to the situation with immediate action.

Taken together, these four steps will allow you to achieve optimal perception, energy management, and performance in any situation.

Before using the SBRT process, you must be familiar with and have practiced the techniques involved in all four steps. The process must become a habit, and the only way to create a habit is to practice. Keep this in mind as we explore the skills you will need in order to master this process.

Stop: Recognizing Personal Signs of Stress

The first step in taking charge of pressure requires recognizing your personal reaction to stress. Once recognized, these personal signs can then serve as cues for engaging in the take-charge approach.

Below is a checklist of changes that occur when a person is experiencing above-optimal levels of pressure. As you read through the checklist, notice symptoms that you have experienced within the last month.

MENTAL CHANGES
- ❏ Problems concentrating
- ❏ Indecisiveness
- ❏ Forgetfulness
- ❏ A racing mind
- ❏ No sense of humor
- ❏ Confusion
- ❏ Rumination
- ❏ Predicting the worst

PHYSICAL CHANGES
- ❏ Constant fatigue
- ❏ Headaches
- ❏ Insomnia
- ❏ Chest pains
- ❏ Tight neck/shoulders
- ❏ A racing heart
- ❏ Heart palpitatons
- ❏ Indigestion

EMOTIONAL CHANGES
- ❏ Irritability
- ❏ Anger
- ❏ Frustration
- ❏ Depression
- ❏ Fear
- ❏ Anxiety
- ❏ Boredom
- ❏ Meaninglessness
- ❏ Feeling ready to explode
- ❏ Feeling powerless
- ❏ Pessimism
- ❏ Unhappy for no reason

BEHAVIORAL CHANGES
- ❏ Increase in nervous habits (e.g., nail biting)
- ❏ Crying for no reason
- ❏ Heavy drinking
- ❏ Procrastination
- ❏ Restlessness
- ❏ Critical of others
- ❏ Inability to get things done
- ❏ Swearing
- ❏ Losing touch with friends

✦ SBRT Exercise—Step 1: STOP

1. Think of the last time you felt pressure at work. Write down the events surrounding this situation.

2. Now think of another time you felt pressure at work. Write down the events surrounding this second situation.

3. For each situation, list the symptoms from the checklist above that you experienced. Were the symptoms similar across situations? If so, these are the symptoms of pressure that are personal to you. If not, try the exercise again and look for commonalities across the situations.

By identifying your personal cues for pressure, you will be in a better position to "stop" when having a stress response. The key is to notice the cues as soon as possible and then literally pause what you are doing, even if for just a moment. Later, we will describe techniques to help you voluntarily stop and assess your symptoms.

Breathe: Engaging in Deep Breathing

Many of the symptoms of stress are part of our natural "fight or flight" response—the automatic physiological arousal that occurs when a situation has been perceived as threatening. As was mentioned previously, we often need this extra boost of energy and the resources it creates to deal effectively with the situation at hand. At the same time, if this extra boost is unnecessary (due to a misperception) or just above optimal, it is a waste of energy.

Engaging in deep breathing keeps stress from spiraling out of control; it also increases energy and alertness. How does it do that? First, we need to understand that the natural response to stress is a shortening of breath —a minimizing of it. This contributes to the spiraling stress and loss of control. The spiral is created by a feedback loop between the body and the mind. The body becomes aroused, minimizes breathing, and automatically engages the mind. Typically the mind becomes negative and this further affects the body, creating a

---

✦ SBRT Exercise: Step 2—BREATHE

Imagine yourself in a negative situation at work. What are
you thinking about the situation? How does your body feel as
you think about this situation? Imagine the best possible outcome of that situation. What are your thoughts in the good
scenario? How does your body feel as you think about the
good scenario?

---

larger physiological reaction. This process is the downward spiral of an impaired response to pressure.

More specifically, we are all aware that the mind affects
the body. When the mind is full of negative thoughts, it
creates chaos in the body, such as high blood pressure,
physical tension, and increased heart rate. The reverse
is also true, but not as often addressed. That is, the
state of the body directly affects the mind. When we are
hyper-aroused, our pattern of thinking becomes fearful
and negative. This negative outlook increases how
threatening a situation appears to be and our physiological response continues to rise.

Deep breathing helps us stop the pressure spiral by
lowering our heart rate and blood pressure and reducing
muscle tension. By manipulating the body in this way,
we actually alter the mind. Our physiological response,
at an optimal level rather than an extreme one, allows
us to keep our perceptions accurate and constructive.
The fight or flight response is thus reversed. Again, the

energy you need for the situation at hand will remain, but wasted energy will be minimized. This is a crucial component of optimal energy management.

Breathing and Relaxation Techniques

Here we will look at a number of techniques for deep breathing: diaphragmatic breathing, the relaxation response (mini-relaxation response and mindfulness), the body scan, and mindful movement (mindful progressive relaxation and mindful stretching). Different techniques are more or less appropriate in different situations. Our goal here is to familiarize you with the techniques and to provide you with an opportunity to practice.

Diaphragmatic Breathing

Diaphragmatic breathing can serve as a quick fix in any situation. As noted above, when we are under pressure our breathing is minimized, becoming shallow. Shallow breathing is short, fast, and confined to our upper chest; it deprives the brain of oxygen. To take charge we need to reverse the process by creating breathing that is deep: longer, slower, and fuller, involving the use of the diaphragm and lower abdomen.

Basic Technique. Take a moment to locate your breathing. Is it confined to your upper chest? If so, on your next in-breath, see if you can relax the chest area and move your breathing down into your lower abdomen. When shallow breathing has become a habit, this may not be as easy as it sounds. When attempting the tech-

➤ *Diaphragmatic Breathing: Three Techniques*

Technique 1: On each inhale, try relocating the breath to the lower abdomen. Count each breath silently on the exhale, backward from 10 to 1.

Technique 2: Using the diaphragmatic breathing, during each inhale, count from 1 to 4; during each exhale count from 4 to 1.

Technique 3: Practice slowing and lengthening the diaphragmatic breath. This can be done by increasing the length of your exhale. During each breath, breathe in for a count of 4, hold the breath for a count of 5, and breathe out, creating an exhale which lasts for a count of 7.

nique for the first time, it is often useful to lie on the floor. When you relax your chest, on the in-breath, your lower abdomen should move out and your diaphragm should move down toward your pelvis. On the out-breath, the abdomen moves in and the diaphragm moves up toward your chest. This series of movements contrasts with breathing that only engages the chest (rising and falling).

The Relaxation Response

The relaxation response, developed by Herbert Benson, M.D., is a counter-mechanism to the physiological state of fight or flight. There are many techniques that elicit the relaxation response. We will focus on two: the mini-relaxation response and mindfulness.

The Mini-Relaxation Response

The most popular technique for eliciting the relaxation response is the mini-relaxation response with a focus on the breath. This response involves four components:

- A quiet environment
- A comfortable position
- The repetition of a simple mental stimulus; here, that stimulus is the breath
- A passive mental attitude

Basic Technique. Shut your office door and sit on the edge of your chair with your hands on your knees and your feet flat on the floor. Focus your attention on your breathing. Do not regulate or try to control it; do not think about it, either. Instead, simply notice that you are breathing, attending to the experience of it (how it feels, the sensations that are occurring). When your attention wanders (as it always will, for that is the nature of the mind), simply acknowledge that it has wandered ("Oh, there goes a thought—it's the nature of the mind to wander"), and then turn your attention back on your breathing. Continue to engage in this refocusing of attention for at least 3 minutes and up to 20 minutes.

The two key aspects of this technique are the repetition of a simple mental stimulus and the passive mental attitude. The repetition focuses your attention on the experience of breathing and helps you refocus when your mind wanders. The passive mental attitude keeps you to simply acknowledging when the mind has wandered and allows you to return to your focus on breathing. Again, you do not want to think about the fact that you are breathing; you want to attend to experience of breathing and refocus your attention on that experience if you find yourself lost in thought.

Mindfulness

The definition of mindfulness is experiencing what you are doing as you do it, moment to moment. The task here is to perform one action at a time and bring your attention to what you are experiencing as you perform that action. The beauty of mindfulness is that it induces the relaxation response without requiring that you take a time-out from tasks, as does the mini-relaxation response. You can practice mindfulness at any time and in any environment. It has two key components:

- A full awareness of what you are experiencing
- A passive attitude toward distracting thoughts

Basic Technique. The easiest method is to focus your attention on the sensations occurring in your body as you perform a task. Just as with the mini-relaxation response, when your mind wanders, you label it "thinking" and then simply refocus your attention on the experience of the task at hand. While you are performing this technique, it is important to give up the goal of relaxing. Relaxation will be a natural consequence of the attention focus.

Mindfulness requires practice, so try it as often as possible. The following exercises will help you.

> ➤ *Mindfulness Exercises*

Mindful Sitting. As you sit working on your computer, notice how your feet feel on the floor or how hard or soft your chair feels. Next, try experiencing the movements of your hands and fingers as they move across the keyboard. It is important not to judge any thoughts that enter your mind. If you find yourself lost in thought (this will likely happen), just acknowledge that you are thinking and refocus your attention on the sensations you are having as you have them.

Mindful Eating. As you eat, focus on all the sensations associated with eating: how the food smells, how the food feels in your mouth, your thoughts about food, your impulse to swallow, sensations of chewing, and so forth.

Mindful Walking. You might practice this as you walk down the hall at work or walk to and from your car. While walking, notice how your body feels as you pick up one foot and put down the other. Notice the swing of your arms and how your clothing feels.

The common element of the mini-relaxation response and mindfulness is the ability to refocus your attention on one thing, whatever is happening in the present moment. The better you can catch yourself when you are lost in thought and refocus your attention, the more successful you will be at inducing the relaxation response.

The next technique, the body scan, will help you develop the skill of experiencing what is happening in your body and so may be useful to your practice of mindfulness.

The Body Scan

The body scan involves sequentially attending to areas of the body and feeling the sensations that arise. When you are engaging in the body scan, simply feel what you are feeling and make no attempt to change the sensations. This is very important, for focusing attention in this way creates the relaxation response.

Basic Technique. Take a moment to follow these steps:

1. Sit on the edge of your chair with your spine erect, as if someone is pulling up on a string attached to the top back of your head. Rest your hands on your knees and set your feet flat on the floor.

2. Starting with your feet, notice the sensations you are having. How do your feet feel upon the floor? Can you feel any clothing touching your feet? Do you feel any sensations of hot or cold or pressure in your feet? What does the sensation really feel like? Be careful not to "think about" the sensations you are having. Instead, just feel them. Do this for at least 30 seconds and up to 1 minute.

3. Now move your attention to your calves. Focus on any sensations you having in your calves, repeating the process used in step 2.

4. Continue to repeat the process, spending at least 30 seconds on each major body part as you move up the body—from calves to thighs, buttocks, back, chest, hands, arms, neck, shoulders, head.

5. When you have finished focusing on the sensations in your head, shift your attention back down to your lower abdomen and engage in deep breathing before moving on with your day.

As in the relaxation response techniques, if your mind wanders, simply acknowledge that it has done so and refocus your attention on the sensations of your body.

Mindful Movement

If pressure has become chronic, we can combine mindfulness and direct movement techniques to reduce tension in the body. This is a two-pronged attack on pressure. Negative emotions such as fear, anxiety, and anger make your muscles contract, and suppressing these feelings only leads to increased tension in the body. Movement directly offsets the bodily tension while mindful attention produces the relaxation response.

Remember that the state of the body directly affects the mind. By manipulating the body, we can maintain an optimal physiological response to pressure and accurate, constructive perceptions. Two techniques that combine mindfulness and movement are mindful progressive relaxation and mindful stretching.

Mindful Progressive Relaxation

Mindful progressive relaxation refers to systematically tensing and releasing all the muscles in your body while attending to the sensations you are having as you progress through this. Progressive relaxation was developed through research on stress and relaxation by Edmund Jacobson, M.D.

Basic Technique. The steps for this technique are as follows:

1. Sit comfortably on the edge of a chair with your spine straight, as if someone is pulling up on a string attached to the top back of your head. Rest your hands on your knees and set your feet flat on the floor.

2. Start with your face. Tense and release its muscles as you breathe, focusing your attention on the sensations you are having. Specifically, on the inhale, tense your face and hold the breath for 5 seconds; on the exhale, release the muscles of your face.

3. Now shift your attention to the neck and shoulders. On the inhale, tense and contract your neck and shoulders muscles and hold the breath for 5 seconds. On the exhale, release the muscles.

4. Repeating this pattern of tensing on the inhale and relaxing on the exhale, progress through the muscle groups of your body (from neck and shoulders to arms, hands, chest, back, waist, buttocks, thighs, calves, ankles, and feet). As you do this, try not to tense any area of the body other than that of your current focus.

Mindful Stretching

Mindful stretching is similar to yoga but its stretches can be incorporated into the workday. The techniques given here are designed for mindful stretching in a chair.

Basic Technique. Sit in a chair. Choose a set of muscles to stretch (see techniques below). Try to attend to the sensations you are having as the stretch is occurring. In addition, engage in deep breathing during the stretch.

➤ *Mindful Stretching: Five Techniques*

STRETCHING THE NECK

1. Place your right hand down by your side, turn the fingers toward your body, and sit on the hand. Relax the shoulder and lean slightly to the left, allowing the head to drop to the left (ear to shoulder). You should feel a stretch in the right side of the neck and the right shoulder. Take three deep breaths in this position.

2. Next, drop the chin toward the chest about 1 inch and take three more deep breaths. Again, drop the chin toward the chest about 1 inch and take three more deep breaths. Allow the chin to fall all the way down to the chest and slowly pick up the head.

3. Repeat on the other side.

STRETCHING THE SHOULDERS AND UPPER CHEST

1. On the inhale, feel like you are breathing into your upper back. Lift the shoulders. Holding the breath, move both shoulders straight back by squeezing your shoulder blades together.

2. On the exhale, keep squeezing the shoulder blades together and pull them down your back until your shoulders are down. Do not stick out your chin as you pull your shoulder blades down.

Techniques Continued

3. Relax the arms and shoulders.

Repeat the above five times.

STRETCHING THE ARMS AND WRIST

1. Extend one hand in front of you with the palm facing the ceiling. The elbow should remain straight throughout this stretch.

2. Stretch the fingers of the hand and bend them toward the floor. With the other hand, very gently pull the fingers back toward your body. Hold for 1 minute and breathe into the areas of the arm and hand that feel tight.

3. Repeat on the other side.

STRETCHING THE WAIST

1. Cross your right leg over your left, with the ankle of the right leg resting on the left knee. Flex the right foot.

2. Turning to the right, place your left hand on the right knee. Place your right hand on the chair behind you. Keeping your head in line with the center of your body, inhale and attempt to stretch toward the ceiling; on the exhale, attempt to turn further around toward the back of the room.

3. Continue for five deep breaths.

4. Repeat on the other side.

STRETCHING THE HIPS AND LEGS

1. Cross the right leg over the left leg, with the ankle of the right leg resting on the left knee. Flex the right foot.

2. Place your hands on the desk in front of you or on your crossed leg. Lean forward until you feel a stretch. Allow gravity to pull your head forward, and just hang your head.

3. Remain in position for five breaths.

4. Repeat on the other side.

✦ SBRT Exercise: The Effects of Mindfulness

Pick any mindfulness technique (mindful sitting, eating, walking; the body scan; progressive relaxation; or stretching). Before practicing the technique, ask yourself: *How does my body feel? What is the state of my mind?*

After answering these questions, practice the technique you have chosen. When your practice is over, again ask: *How does my body feel? What is the state of my mind?*

The Importance of Practice

The more you practice the techniques, the sooner the second SBRT step, Breathe, will become an automatic reaction to pressure: a habit. That habit will pay off for you in the time and energy you gain from controlling your stress response.

Although these techniques are simple and require little time, most individuals will not use them without some type of training. This is because people tend to believe they will get more done if they "just keep working." They fail to realize that the physical tension that accumulates when we "just keep working" leads to an above-optimal physiological response, which translates into a waste of time and energy. Indeed, most of us are unaware of the time and energy we devote to tension and non-adaptive responses to pressure. By practicing the "Breathe" techniques, though, we will see a difference and have the energy we need to make the most efficient use of the SBRT steps.

Why is habit replacement so important? Because when we are under pressure, we tend to rely on habit. Our body and mind naturally want to work as efficiently as possible, and habits are easy for us—they are the behaviors that require the least amount of effort. Our goal is thus to develop the entire SBRT approach as a habit. Once done, when pressure arises, we will automatically deal with it an advantageous way. Later in this pocket guide, we will further explore how to establish SBRT as a habit.

CHAPTER 6

Optimal Perception: Rewrite

ONCE WE HAVE acknowledge a sign of stress such as tension or irritability, we practice the first two SBRT steps, Stop and Breathe; then we move on to the important third step, Rewrite. In this step, we reflect upon the situation at hand and assess whether or not we have accurately perceived the situation as threatening. If we have not, we modify our perception. As mentioned earlier, stress involves our interpretation of the event. Often, our perceptions are inaccurate or exaggerated; they do not accord with reality. Our physiology, however, makes no distinction between what is real and what is perceived. What is perceived is real to the body. Thus, perceiving the situation optimally is crucial.

In order to rewrite, we need to understand that a thought is just a thought. Most of us automatically believe what we think. This can have unfortunate consequences when what we think is untrue, negative, or not in our best interest. If you think, "Wow, I am really a loser," you will immediately have a physiological response to the statement. Because the statement is untrue, the physiological response is a waste of energy. Every thought we have generates a physiological response. When that thought is not in our best interest, it contributes to our physiology spiraling out of control.

Research has shown that when we feel pressure, our thoughts and self-talk (the statements we make to ourselves) tend to become inaccurate. Pressure leads us to interpret ambiguous stimuli negatively. For example, imagine that you have sent an email to your boss outlining a new project you would like to complete. Your boss does not respond all day. This situation is ambiguous, but pressure will likely bias you to interpret the situation negatively: "My boss must not like the idea and is looking for a way to let me down easy." Complicating the situation, studies show that our brain (whether under pressure or not) is biased toward negativity, responding more strongly to negative stimuli then to positive stimuli. All this negative thinking has two consequences:

1. The negative focus diverts attention and energy from dealing with the task at hand; it thus reduces efficiency and productivity.

2. For every negative thought, there is a negative physiological reaction; this reaction culminates in a non-adaptive stress response.

When we are experiencing pressure, we should automatically question our self-statements and beliefs. If we can make an accurate assessment and divide what needs to be addressed from what is just a misperception, then an adaptive response will follow. We can choose our viewpoint and respond in an optimal way to stress.

Thought Distortions and Irrational Beliefs

Before we look at the process of rewriting, it is important to lay out the typical pressure-related inaccuracies that our minds produce. The list below presents several common thought distortions (Burns, 1989). Once we begin to recognize these as misperceptions, we can address them as they arise and replace them with accurate perceptions of the situation. As you read through the list, see if you can remember a time when you yourself engaged in this type of thinking.

- All-or-nothing thinking—Thinking in black-and-white terms
- Overgeneralization—Generalizing from one situation to all situations
- Mental filter—Picking out and dwelling upon one negative detail of an otherwise good experience
- Jumping to conclusions—Concluding the worst when the worst is not substantiated by facts
- Emotional reasoning—Using emotional statements as evidence of the truth
- Magnification—Exaggerating the significance of a negative event

- Personalization—Assuming responsibility for a negative event when it is not your responsibility
- Blame—Blaming others when it is inappropriate

Irrational beliefs may underlie or fuel these distortions, and are often the cause of maladaptive behavior and thinking. Such beliefs are subtle—often "unconscious" —and so can escape our detection even as they drive our behavior. Their irrationality is rooted in the extent to which they are held and under what circumstances. For instance, seeking approval is perfectly appropriate in many situations, but expecting approval in all situations can lead to maladaptive thinking and conflict.

Here is a more specific example: Imagine you have given a presentation and your manager's response is "I enjoyed your presentation, but your slides could have been more engaging." The maladaptive, automatic train of thought might be: "I should have constructed the slides differently; therefore, the presentation was bad; therefore, the people who said nice things were only being kind; therefore, they don't think the presentation was good; therefore, the presentation was terrible; therefore, no one approves of me or my work." The basis of such a train of thought—the irrational belief that one should be able to obtain approval in all situations—thus results in severe distortion and an overall negative feeling about the situation. Again, such beliefs, despite their powerful effect on us, often escape our conscious notice.

> ➤ *Typical Irrational Beliefs*

- I must have love and approval from family, friends, and peers.
- I must be perfect in all I undertake.
- Certain people are evil and should be punished.
- It is horrible when things are not the way you would like them to be.
- External events cause human misery.
- You should fear the unknown, the uncertain, or the potentially dangerous.
- It is easier to avoid life's difficulties and responsibilities than to face them.
- You need something stronger or greater than you to rely on.
- The past primarily determines the present.
- Happiness can be achieved by inaction, passivity, and endless leisure.

✦ SBRT Exercise: Thought Distortions and Irrational Beliefs

Think of the last time that you felt negative about a work situation. What thoughts were running through your mind at the time? Can you explain any of those thoughts as stemming from thought distortions or irrational beliefs? How did you behave directly after the incident? How might you reinterpret or re-approach that situation?

Rewrite: Perceiving the Situation Optimally

Obviously, few of us have time to think about a list of thought distortions and irrational beliefs when we are in a pressure situation; thus, the goal is to become so familiar with these distortions and beliefs that you can recognize them when they occur. It is also important, when in any situation, to tune in to your self-talk and recognize there is always more than one way of viewing things. How do you do this? For each thought, ask yourself at least two questions: *What is the evidence for this?* and *Are these statements in my best interest?* At first you may need to write out your thoughts, but later this process will come to you more automatically.

To practice rewriting, follow these four steps:

1. **Notice automatic thoughts.** In any situation we need to tune in and listen to what we are saying to ourselves. Instead of talking to yourself on auto-pilot, notice the words and ideas being expressed.

2. **Identify distortions.** See if you recognize any thought distortions or irrational beliefs. Typical words to watch out for are *should, must, have to, ought, always,* and *never.*

3. **Challenge thoughts.** Ask yourself: *What is the evidence for this? Is there another way to view this situation? Is it in my best interest to hold this belief?*

4. **Rewrite thoughts.** Talk back to yourself with positives and replace the thought distortions and irrational beliefs with more accurate, constructive statements. If you do not have enough evidence to weigh in on an idea, take action and look for the evidence.

➤ *From Distortion to Positive Self-Talk: Examples*

THOUGHTS	REWRITES
I made the wrong decision on the Anderson account.	There's no evidence that the decision was incorrect—it's too soon to know.
My boss hates me.	He's simply under pressure himself right now and in a bad mood.
There's nothing I can do about my work overload.	My work overload is daunting, but I can handle it if I do [such and such].
I'm the only one who doesn't understand this.	There's evidence that others don't understand it either. I'll propose that we ask for better directions.
I should be able to finish this project more quickly.	There's no proof that I should be able to do that.
I'm stupid.	I did well in college, and if anyone else said I was stupid, I'd know it was untrue. I'm capable of doing this job.

✦ WORKSHEET:
Rewriting for Optimal Perception

Directions: Answer the questions below to practice rewriting.

1. Write down the last event that led to a stressful state of mind at work. Be sure to detail the situation.

2. What was your emotional response to the event? What specific thoughts accompanied that emotional response?

3. Return to the thoughts above and examine them, looking for thought distortion or irrationality. Rewrite the thoughts with something more accurate or more useful.

4. How do you feel when you read the new responses?

• *Worksheet Concluded*

In rewriting, keep in mind that all thoughts are just thoughts. It will help you avoid the pitfall of self-criticism, especially if you are the type of person who tends to obsess over evaluating self-performance. In such a case, be extra careful to ask the right questions and not to criticize your lack of ability to perceive the situation optimally. In short, don't beat yourself up for beating yourself up.

For instance, let us say your boss is not entirely un-happy with something you did. You find yourself think-ing, "I can't do anything right"; then you realize this is the thought distortion of all-or-nothing thinking—a real-ization that prompts the self-critical statement "I can't even stop these negative, distorted thoughts!" Clearly, this will only worsen the situation, fueling your negative train of thought. Thus take care to acknowledge that a thought is just a thought and move on to correcting your perceptions.

As we have seen in this chapter, our automatic percep-tion of a situation as threatening may be inaccurate, requiring us to rewrite our internal dialog. Because our physiology makes no distinction between perception and reality, perceiving the situation optimally is crucial to preventing a stress response that spirals out of control. We need to notice our automatic thoughts and identify the presence of any thought distortions or irrational be-liefs; then we need to challenge those ideas and rewrite our self-talk with more accurate, useful information.

CHAPTER 7

Optimal Performance: Take Action

AFTER WE STOP, breathe, and rewrite, it is time for the fourth step in the SBRT process: Take Action. In taking action, we resolve the situation at hand. There are a number of steps for choosing a plan of action. At first, you may need to write out your options, but later this process will come to you more automatically.

Taking Action: Resolving the Situation

The step of taking action involves the following:

1. Identifying the problem to be solved
2. Generating and assessing possible solutions
3. Choosing a solution
4. Designing a plan of action
5. Doing something in your plan, even if it is only a small component

Keep in mind that doing something in your plan is the best way to ensure optimal energy management.

The Importance of Identifying the Problem

To take action, we need to see whether or not rewriting allowed us to separate the problem at hand from the "emotional hook"—the automatic thoughts that accompany a problem and obscure it. Emotional hooks escalate problems and interfere with our finding solutions to them. Sometimes it is the hook that needs addressing, not the situation. As the point of taking action is to deal with the problem itself (if necessary), we must define both it and the emotional hook if rewriting has not clarified the problem.

The following is a situation that requires separating the problem from the emotional hook. You have been waiting all day to meet with your boss and colleagues about a presentation scheduled for tomorrow. As your appointment time approaches, his secretary tells you that the meeting has been cancelled and that you should finalize the presentation on your own. You react angrily towards the secretary, your heart starts racing, and you begin to worry about whether the presentation will be up to par. Soon you are also brooding about the fact that you always keep your appointments, so others should do so as well. You leave work feeling upset and remain that way until late into the evening.

What is the problem and what is the emotional hook?

- Let us say that before giving a presentation, you have always obtained group feedback on your

presentation material. You thus expected feedback from your boss and colleagues at the meeting; in fact, you were relying on it.

- Let us also say that your automatic train of
thought ran something like this: "The boss is incon-
siderate and unreliable. What if I make a fool of
myself during the presentation? What if my pitch
falls flat? I always rearrange my schedule for
other people, but they never rearrange it for me.
Jones got his meeting; why didn't I get mine?"

Clearly, the problem is that you wanted the feedback
and were relying on it. The emotional hook—replete with
feelings of denial, self-doubt, and unfairness—did nothing but obscure the problem and worsen the situation.
By separating the problem from the emotional hook, you
are now in a better position to deal with the problem.

Problem Solving, Action Planning, and Doing

The balance of the Take Action process involves the
following:

- **Finding a solution to the problem.** To do this,
take these steps:
  — First, identify as many possible solutions as
  you can.
  — Next, consider the possibilities, listing the pros
  and cons for each solution.
  — Finally, choose the most acceptable solution.

- **Planning for action.** Once you have chosen a solution, write up a plan of action. Be sure to divide the plan into reasonable, doable steps. At that time, *take action.*

- **Taking action.** Immediately do something, even if what you have chosen to do is only a small step.

For instance, let us return to the example above, in which you relied on feedback for your presentation. You might come up with these possibilities for solving the problem:

- As your boss is leaving work, explain the situation to get a meeting early the next morning.

- Appeal to the secretary, explaining the weight of the situation and attempting to get her to talk the boss into rescheduling a meeting.

- Enlist a group of coworkers and meet without the boss.

- Enlist one trusted colleague to critique the work.

- Go with what you have done and hope it works out.

Of the possible solutions, which seems the most practical and doable? To answer this question, you would list pros and cons for each solution. Next, you would decide which option has the most acceptable combination of pros and cons. Here, you might pick enlisting a trusted friend to critique the work because it provides the pros of obtaining feedback but only requires arrangements involving one person; the only con is making time for this prior to the presentation.

Now a written plan of action is in order. It should consist of small doable steps that include something that can be done immediately. For instance, to return to our example, let us say that, for various reasons, you decided to enlist a group of coworkers to critique the work. You might make this plan:

1. Write an email requesting an audience to critique your presentation sometime between now and three hours before the presentation.
2. Send the email to a number of people.
3. Once they reply, set up the meeting.
4. If no one replies before a certain time of day, move to calling individuals at home.
5. If phone calls are necessary, create a phone list.

Writing the email is a simple, doable step that gets the ball rolling toward solving the problem.

As we have seen in this chapter, Step 4 of the SBRT process is to take action. The process involves identifying the problem to be solved, generating and assessing possible solutions, choosing a solution, and designing a plan of action. Finally, the best way to ensure optimal energy management is to do something in your plan, even if it is only a small component.

CHAPTER 8

Making SBRT a Habit

BEFORE APPLYING the SBRT technique to specific situations, we need to understand that this technique must become a habit—one that replaces mismanaged pressure. As mentioned earlier, habit replacement is important because we tend to rely on habit when under pressure. Our body and mind naturally want to work as efficiently as possible. Habits are habits because they are easy for us; they are the behavior that requires the least amount of effort. Our goal is thus to develop the Stop, Breathe, Rewrite, and Take Action approach as a habit. In this way, when pressure arises, our habit will be to deal with it advantageously.

Keep in mind that performing well under pressure will not miraculously occur simply because you have read this book. It requires practice and persistence both when you are under pressure and when you are not. The latter is particularly important, for if you have not tried to develop these behaviors as a habit during less stressful times, you may create cognitive overload try-ing to develop them when stress is high. If a workshop or training manual on performing under pressure only provides information for use when you are already on overload, nothing will change; in fact, pressure will be increased. It is therefore vital, from the start, to work at establishing the SBRT technique as a habit. Once established, performing well under pressure will be somewhat automatic and require little response effort.

Developing the SBRT Habit: Key Steps

To develop the habit of performing well under pressure, *each day* follow these key steps:

1. Remind yourself of the importance of habit replacement, that is, breaking the habit of mismanaged pressure and establishing the SBRT habit.
2. Use cueing to "check in" and practice.
3. Reward yourself for success.

I. Remind Yourself of the Importance of Habit Replacement

In this first step, remind yourself of what you will gain from breaking the habit of mismanaged pressure. Keep in mind that we habitually respond to pressure in a non-optimal way because of its short-term payoff—we see that being under stress can help us get the job done. Yet, such stress often spirals out of control, lowering productivity in the long run and creating a need for

---

> **➤ Your Personal Reminder**

- By performing well under pressure, I will increase my productivity. If I were more productive, I would feel:

- By performing well under pressure, I will have more time to get things done. If I had extra time, I would:

- By performing well under pressure, I will increase my level of energy. If I had more energy, I would:

- By performing well under pressure, I will be able to relax when I leave work. If I were relaxed when I left work, I would:

"recovery time." This is why you need to constantly remind yourself of the long-term payoff of performing well under pressure. Specifically, remind yourself that when you channel the physiological boost associated with stress in the correct way, your productivity will increase, you will feel energized, and you will not require recovery time.

Above is a handy personal reminder. Complete the open-ended statements and keep the reminder in an easily accessible place in your desk. Look it over each time you have reason to be in that area of your desk.

2. Use Cueing to "Check In" and Practice

This second step in developing the SBRT habit serves as an early warning system as well as a way to practice stress management. You want to catch the symptoms of pressure (both physical and psychological) as early as possible to offset any negative stress reaction; you also want to practice the SBRT process as often as possible.

Specifically, create one or more cues that you will use throughout the day to "check in" on your stress levels. Use the cues for practice whether you are under pressure or not.

In general, follow these two guidelines:

- If you are under pressure, use the cue to complete the entire SBRT process.

- If you are not under pressure, use the cue to engage in the first two steps, Stop and Breathe. This will promote optimal energy management and make performing under pressure much easier when the need arises.

Suggestions and techniques for incorporating cueing into your workday are detailed on the following page. They focus on "Waiting Time," "The Usual Routine," and "Your Environment."

> ## ➤ *Incorporating Cueing Into Your Workday*

WAITING TIME

Use waiting time as a cue; for example, when you are waiting in traffic, in line, for your computer to respond, and for a phone call. "Check in" and practice breathing and mindfulness techniques instead of becoming impatient and angry.

Preparing to use this cue: Write down three common workday situations in which you must wait. What is your usual response in these situations? Which breathing technique is most natural to you and can be done in the situations likely to arise?

THE USUAL ROUTINE

"Check in" and practice mindfulness during your usual routine. For example, practice when walking to and from your car, before starting a new task, or when preparing to make an important phone call. During your next workday, mindfully perform a routine activity.

Preparing to use this cue: Pick three common actions you perform multiple times during your workday. What is your usual response to these situations? Do you perform the actions without thought? To remind yourself to perform mindfully, record the actions on Post-Its and hang them near the place of activity. For example, put one in your car that reads "Walk mindfully to your destination."

YOUR ENVIRONMENT

Environmental cues include a phone ringing, email arriving, and someone saying hello. Take these as opportunities to practice deep breathing. For example, when the phone rings, take two deep breaths before picking up the receiver.

Preparing to use this cue: Pick three environmental cues. What is your usual response to these situations? Decide to use them as opportunities to practice deep breathing. Record the cues on a Post-It labeled "Breathe" so that you do not forget.

3. Reward Yourself for Success

As we have seen, one reason why mismanaged tension becomes a habit is that we get an immediate reward from it. The fact is, as much as we hate to admit it, everyone performs for rewards. We repeat behaviors that "get us something," and will stop doing whatever is not rewarded. One basic law of reward systems is that immediate rewards are more effective (or more rewarding) than delayed rewards.

Consider the following choices:

- Smoking a cigarette and feeling better in the moment versus not smoking a cigarette and living longer

- Eating ice cream for dessert because it tastes good versus eating yogurt and keeping your weight down in the long run

- Shouting at someone in anger and feeling a release of tension versus controlling your anger and not saying something that will ruin your future friendship

- Working though dinner to get a project finished versus how you will feel for the rest of the evening

Clearly, when we have a choice between a small immediate reward and a large delayed reward, we tend to choose the former. Think of a child who is offered the choice between getting one bag of M&Ms today or two bags of M&Ms tomorrow. Every child will take the single bag of M&Ms today. You are probably thinking, *But how does this apply to me? I'm not a child! If I can make one million dollars today but two million dollars if I wait until tomorrow, I'll wait until tomorrow!*

The problem is, most of us, especially when under pressure, fail to think of the larger, delayed reward; instead, we fall back on habit and choose the smaller, immediate reward. For instance, if you didn't know or hadn't considered that you could make two million dollars tomorrow, you would take one million today. This is not because you are acting like a child but because you haven't really considered the larger, delayed reward.

The majority of us suffer from the habit of performing sub-optimally under pressure. The short-term rewards —particularly the feeling that we're getting the job done—reinforce this habit. Yet if we stop and look at the bigger picture, we find that the rewards of managing stress with SBRT are, in the long term, much greater: Not only will we get the job done, but our work will be of higher quality, we will feel energized, and we will be ready to approach the next project more quickly. Dealing with delayed gratification is partly why it is so important to remind yourself of the rewards of engaging in the SBRT process. Along with this reminder, though, you should consciously provide yourself with more immediate reinforcement—short-term rewards for engaging in the process.

There are many techniques for developing immediate rewards. The use of multiple techniques simultaneously is optimal. Here are six possibilities:

- **Keep track of your success.** During the day, keep a record of how many times you engaged in the SBRT technique. Simply being aware of your actions can serve as reinforcement. For example: Create a table on your computer, and checkmark the table each time you engage in the SBRT technique. Be sure to keep the table in a visible place.

- **Use tangible rewards.** Decide on a reward-contingency system. For example, if you engage in SBRT three times in one day, reward yourself with 20 minutes of web-surfing or a special coffee drink. The reward should be something that you enjoy and are willing to sacrifice if you fail to meet your daily goal. Be careful not to choose rewards that will promote more stress or otherwise work against you. For instance, do not use alcohol or staying up incredibly late as a reward; either will make you tired and unfocused.

- **Reflect on the positive things that you accomplished today.** At the end of the day, take a moment, breathe deep, and reflect on the positive things that have happened. Examples of positive things include projects that got finished, good conversations with coworkers, and the fact that you aren't extremely stressed-out.

- **Use self-praise.** Immediately after engaging in the SBRT technique, praise yourself. For example, say something nice such as "Way to go" or "I'm on the ball today."

- **Notice the way your body feels.** The SBRT technique has the natural reinforcing property of reducing stress and tension. Tune in to your body and see how it feels. With some practice, you should be able to notice a big difference.

- **Have another person provide the reinforcement.** Keep track of your success by joining forces with a partner. In this way, the two of you can reinforce each other and supply praise. It is much easier to maintain reinforcement contingencies if another person is involved in the process.

As we have seen in this chapter, to use the SBRT technique effectively, you must establish it as a habit. To create the habit, you need to remind yourself of the delayed reward of engaging in SBRT, use cueing to "check in" with yourself throughout the day, and provide yourself with immediate rewards for practice.

CHAPTER 9

Dealing With Time Pressure

AS WE HAVE SEEN, performing well under pressure requires the four basic steps of SBRT: Stop, Breathe, Rewrite, and Take Action. To review:

- **Stop** refers to noticing and then interrupting mental and physical cues that you are under pressure.

- **Breathe** means to engage in deep breathing or mindfulness in order to counteract the automatic physiological response to pressure and keep it under control.

- **Rewriting** involves noticing and challenging thought distortions in order to create an accurate perception of the situation at hand.

- Finally, **taking action** refers to the use of a problem-solving approach to respond to the situation with immediate action.

In the remaining chapters of this pocket guide, we will describe how to practice and apply these steps in commonly stressful workplace situations. In particular, we will focus on the following five situational stressors:

1. Time
2. Anger
3. People
4. Fatigue
5. Evaluation

We begin in this chapter with the first stressor: time.

Time Pressure

Are you constantly living by a calendar, doing two things at once, checking your watch, and becoming overly irritated when you must do such things as wait in line? These are signs that you are feeling the pressure of time. Many workers feel this pressure on a daily basis.

Take Moe, for instance. On a typical day, he has three meetings in the morning and a presentation to give in the afternoon. He also must answer important emails and finish several reports. Today promises to be typical until Moe gets stuck in traffic on the way to work. Not wanting to cancel his first meeting, he tries to cut ahead of other cars. The difficulty of this makes him so angry, he's still cursing under his breath as he gets to work—where his assistant promptly reports that the first meeting has been set back 20 minutes. "Why did you allow that?" Moe yells at her. "This disrupts my entire day! Reschedule my second meeting so I'll have enough time for the first!"

Off to his office Moe goes, to sort through endless email. Each trivial email makes his chest and neck muscles grow tighter. He finds an email that he missed yesterday requiring that a certain report be finished by 1:00 PM today. Realizing that this makes lunch impossible, Moe leaves for his meeting, and then discovers he's a few minutes early. During the wait, he obsesses about what he could be getting done in his office. By the time the others arrive, he finds himself saying, "Wow, my watch must be fast—I feel like I've been waiting for an hour. Let's finally get to this meeting." His colleagues look offended by his remarks. Needless to say, by 9:15 AM, Moe already feels as if his day is ruined.

There were many opportunities for Moe to turn his day around, but like most of us when under time pressure, all he could think about was getting everything done. Unfortunately, the "get everything done" approach leads to an impaired stress response. Once that happens, you will feel pressure even if you do meet all your responsibilities. To ward off such a response, you need to notice the cues of time pressure and engage in the SBRT technique as you try to finish your responsibilities.

I. Stop

Common cues for stopping when under time pressure include irritability, anger, general discontent, feeling ready to explode, constantly checking your watch, headache, tight neck and shoulders, concentration problems, and careless errors in speech, writing, or movement.

As soon as one of these symptoms arises, *stop.*

You must consciously choose to do one thing at a time. Focus only on the task in front of you. Multi-tasking, or dividing your attention, only allows you to do the same number of things in the same amount of time at a lower level of quality. Even computers freeze up when there are too many operations being performed. Instead, choose one task and focus fully on that task.

2. Breathe

When we are under time pressure, it always seems impossible to set aside time to gain control of the situation. Because of this, the best approach is to engage in deep breathing and mindfulness while you work. Both can be performed as you continue to complete your objectives.

One of the most frustrating forms of time pressure is being forced to wait for something or someone. Ironically, waiting can actually be a stroke of good luck. Instead of viewing this downtime as a problem, see it as an opportunity to engage in deep breathing and mindfulness.

For example, look at Moe. Instead of trying to cut ahead in traffic, he could have used the wait to engage in deep breathing; if he had, he would have arrived at work feeling in control and better able to deal with his assistant's news—his bullying response might have been replaced by a problem-solving interaction. He also could have engaged in deep breathing while waiting for others to arrive for the meeting; if he had, it is likely he would have greeted his colleagues appropriately and have had something constructive to say.

3. Rewrite

Time pressure results in "overload mode." Overload mode is a general negative feeling, such as distress. It is marked by low confidence, a low sense of control, and many negative thoughts. The rewriting process is thus quite important when you are under time pressure. Remember:

- First, notice your automatic thoughts; be on the lookout for self-talk that includes *must, have to,* and *should* statements.

- Next, identify any thought distortions, such as all-or-nothing thinking and jumping to conclusions. If you notice any of these, challenge their validity.

- Finally, engage in positive self-talk and replacement self-talk.

For example, let us return to Moe. As he was stuck in traffic, he was most likely thinking: "I can't believe this; these drivers are idiots; I have to get to that meeting on time or my whole day is shot; my colleagues will think I'm blowing them off and leave me out of the next project; my assistant better cover for me or she's in trouble" —and so on. Instead of fueling this train of thoughts, Moe could have noticed its exaggerations and distortions, such as "having" to get to the meeting on time and his "whole" day being shot if he is late (this is all-or-nothing thinking); he also could have considered other possibilities, such as calling his assistant and asking her to postpone the meeting for 10 minutes. Moreover, Moe does not really know what his colleagues are thinking or will think, and sets up his assistant for groundless blame.

Through rewriting, Moe can stop the train of negative thoughts; he can admit there is nothing he can do about the traffic, realize that he does not know what his colleagues think, and acknowledge that his assistant will help him when he asks for help.

4. Take Action

When you take action under time pressure, it is critical to prioritize without perfectionism.

First, remind yourself that it is a waste of time to rehash the past and worry about the future; then use mindfulness to focus on the present. Focusing on the present will help relieve feelings of time pressure.

If you must think about the past and plan for the future, plan in the present and remember with full awareness. Sit down and mindfully construct the plan; do not let your thoughts take off on planning activities. Getting the thoughts on paper will allow you to set them aside. Similarly, if you are bombarded with thoughts of the past, write down how those thoughts apply to the current situation and decide if they can contribute to your plans.

Next, see if rewriting helped you separate the emotion from the problem at hand. For example, Moe may have discovered these concrete problems: the possibility that he would be late for the meeting, his lack of a good email-screening device, and the need to finish a report while finding time for lunch. All of Moe's other thoughts and actions were masking solutions to the problems.

Now, find possible solutions for the problem. In general, when you are under time pressure, the main problem is not having enough time. One solution is to eliminate as many demands on your time as possible. To do this, try the following:

- Making a to-do list
- Screening phone calls and emails
- Scheduling work breaks

Making a To-Do List

The best approach is to make your list when you first get to work, before doing anything. There are three steps to this simple technique:

1. Focus on the big picture and list everything that must be completed today.
2. Go through the list and divide it into what you must do, should do, and want to do.

3. Review the "must" and "should" options. In reviewing, (a) reassess to see if you can eliminate a few things, and (b) consider delegating the task to someone else. Be fully aware that you are not the only employee—coworkers can contribute to a task.

If you often find yourself under time pressure, make a to-do list on a daily basis. Again, the best time for this is when you first get to work; if you wait, pressure will accumulate and make planning difficult.

As you complete your listed assignments, make sure you are doing one thing at a time and fully focusing your attention on it. If you habitually think that multi-tasking is the most efficient approach, remember that in the long term it can increase time pressure, lengthening the time spent on tasks and reducing work quality. It can also leave you feeling overwhelmed and thus paralyzed.

Screening Phone Calls and Emails

This is another way to eliminate demands on your time. If a call is really important, the caller will leave a message. If you are worried about offending key players on your team, check your messages at scheduled intervals and call back right away. Find out from your information-technology team how to filter, organize, and prioritize your email.

Scheduling Work Breaks

Create a schedule for your breaks and take them. Pushing through will not allow you to complete more in the long run. Taking a moment to recharge will allow you to complete more quality work and prevent a maladaptive physiological response. Taking short breaks can actually speed up work, resulting in more completed work and less fatigue (Grandjean, 1991).

All in all, in taking action, do not strive for perfection. Perfectionism is a waste of time. There is a difference between quality and perfection. When you find yourself obsessing about a tiny detail, go back to rewriting and question your thinking.

As we have seen in this chapter, many workers feel time pressure on a daily basis. Whenever you are under this kind of pressure, be sure to follow SBRT:

1. Stop—Do one thing at a time.
2. Breathe—Engage in deep breathing and mindfulness regularly and especially when waiting.
3. Rewrite—Change negative thoughts rather than fuel them.
4. Take action—Prioritize without perfectionism.

CHAPTER 10

Dealing With Anger Pressure

ALL OF US get angry at one time or another. Some us get angry every day. We are especially vulnerable to anger when we are under pressure from such things as time, people, and evaluation. Anger itself has pressures, notably the pressure of deciding whether to contain that anger or act on it. In either case, the experience of anger will result in an elevated physiological response. Our task is to direct that energy appropriately and make the physiological boost work for us.

Anger Pressure

Let us think about what anger is and where it comes from. Anger typically has three components:

1. The thought that we have been wronged in some way

2. The physiological reaction of bracing for physical assault—a reaction that includes increased blood pressure and heart rate

3. An attack response: verbal, physical, or otherwise.

— 111 —

The pressure of anger begins with the physiological reaction, which, if not attended to, often results in an attack response. The goal of using the SBRT technique when you are under anger pressure is to regulate the physiological response, prevent an attack, and transform the extra energy into something useful.

I. Stop

Most of the time, we know when we are angry; still, sometimes we must rely on cues. Typical cues for anger are a racing mind, lack of humor, rumination, irritability, cursing, frustration, impulse to bully others, critical attitude toward others, feeling ready to explode, chest pains, headache, tight neck and shoulders, racing heart, and indigestion.

2. Breathe

Anger is typically accompanied by quick, intense physiological arousal. Do not try to avoid the arousal because this will just make it worse; however, you do have to temper the physiological response so that you can deal with the situation at hand. For this, we suggest an approach called "action-distraction." It involves increasing your activity level and focusing your attention on something other than the anger-provoking event. As we have seen, the goal of the Breathe step is to keep your physiological response from spiraling out of control. Here, this step requires active, invigorating techniques rather than passive ones.

Think about the last time you were angry at work. Did you lash out at someone? Did you brood about the situation at your desk? Based on personality, there are two typical responses to anger:

- Lashing out
- Ruminating

Often an anger response will include both of these components.

If you have ever yelled at a coworker for asking you a question or slammed a door in vexation with a situation, you have lashed out. Lashing out is rooted in the quick, intense rise in physiological arousal that accompanies anger. It clouds our judgment and contributes to impulsive behavior. If you tend to lash out, you may get a reputation for abusing others and people will want to avoid you, including important clients.

Ruminating involves constantly rehashing the anger-provoking event in your mind ("I can't believe Bill said that! What right does he have?"). Ruminating usually includes elaborate, dramatic plans for action. These plans are rarely practical; instead, they fuel the anger response and contribute to its out-of-control spiraling.

The Action-Distraction Approach

Both lashing out and ruminating are neutralized by action-distraction:

- Action dissipates the quick arousal associated with anger.

- Distraction keeps you from ruminating and allows you to acquire some distance between the anger you feel and the action you decide to take.

There are Breathe techniques discussed earlier that, with some modification, can be used in action-distraction. For instance:

- Mindful, vigorous exercise. An example of this excellent technique is mindful but brisk walking. Even if you simply walk up and down the stairs or hallway a few times, you will notice a difference in your anger pressure.

- Intense mindful progressive relaxation

The physical action of each exercise will counteract the intense rise in arousal. At the same time, the mindful focus will help you attend to something other than the anger itself. Remember, do not try to use stationary or "relaxing" techniques when you are angry. Unless you have had years of practice, staying in one place and attempting such techniques is usually a mistake. It typically leads to rumination and at worst results in a magnification of the problem.

Anger creates a lot of energy, and you can use it to your benefit. For a distraction method, direct that energy into a task that needs completing, and complete the task mindfully. Choose a simple, straightforward task —anger taxes the resources needed for tackling anything complex, such as a task requiring intense thought and logic. Examples of appropriate tasks include organizing files (e.g., email, paper), taking a walk (e.g., to get water, pick up mail, drop off a report), and leaving or returning phone messages to people not associated with the anger-producing event.

3. Rewrite

Rewrite only after fully engaging in action-distraction, including any Breathe exercises (for instance, rewrite after, not during, a brisk walk). Throughout the rewriting process, try to engage in deep breathing. Just thinking about the situation that made you angry tends to bring back the negative physiological response.

Noticing automatic thoughts and identifying distortions are particularly difficult steps to take when you are angry because the thoughts will tend toward the extreme and you may find enjoyment or satisfaction in thinking about them. To deal with this problem, do the following:

- Try to determine whether the thoughts are truly automatic—you may be consciously fueling them. Sometimes when we are angry, we intentionally create an inner dialog full of thought distortions. It might "feel good" to do this, but will in no way help the situation; so see whether your angry inner voice is fueling your thoughts.

- Identify distortions. These tend to involve a predominantly negative focus on the situation, negative thoughts about others, and an attempt to blame the situation on anyone but oneself.

  In general, be on the alert for distortions such as discounting the positive, blame, mental filtering, emotional reasoning, magnification, and the use of the words *never* and *always.* Be sure to challenge the distortions. Ask, "Is my anger justified?" If you think so, then what is the evidence for this? Even if the anger is justified, ask yourself whether the thoughts are in your best interest. Engage in positive self-talk.

4. Take Action

Make sure that rewriting helped you separate the problem to be solved from the emotional hook. Typically anger arises because an expectation was not met. For instance, we expect to get to work quickly and then run into traffic—an obstacle that contradicts our expectation, thus provoking anger. To deal with anger, then, we must know what we expected. Was it a reasonable expectation? Does the expectation need to be addressed? Identifying the expectation can help clarify the problem to be solved.

Decision: To Communicate or Not

Your first decision is whether or not the situation or problem warrants action on the communication front.

We usually see *someone* as the cause of our anger (whether that person indeed caused it or not). You must decide if you want to communicate with this person or someone else about the situation. Before taking this step, carefully consider whether a confrontation would be appropriate and useful. The confrontation will be useful only if . . .

(a) you are going to express your real feelings about the situation, or

(b) you can express clearly what you need from the person to resolve the situation or prevent it from recurring.

This means taking the time to acquire the answers to (a) and (b).

First, what are your real feelings about the situation? You are obviously angry, but where is that coming from? Typically anger is generated by hurt, betrayal, disapproval, frustration, humiliation, threat, or pain. Getting to the bottom of which emotion is fueling the anger will help you communicate the problem.

Second, discover what you need from the person to resolve the situation. What specific thing can be done or could have been done to eliminate the anger-generating emotion? What thwarted expectation was behind the anger? In this communication, what do you need or expect to get in order to resolve the problem? Be as specific as you can in answering that question. Finally, who can meet this need? The person to approach is the person capable of actually meeting your need.

Choosing to Communicate

If you provided clear, concrete answers to the questions above and decide to communicate, then:

- Be specific about what your expectations were and what the problem was.

- Ask for what you need and suggest specific actions that you feel should be taken.

For example, a good approach is "I feel [specify feelings]. I feel this way because [specify reason]. I need [provide concrete and specific needs]. If possible, in the future could we approach the situation in the following way? [Provide concrete and specific suggestions]."

Choosing Not to Communicate

If you could not provide clear, concrete answers to all the decisive questions, then it is probably inappropriate to engage in an interaction about the situation. Perhaps at this time it is simply not possible to address or change the anger's underlying cause.

In such a case, you need to focus on changing your reaction to the situation. It is important to act in some way, for unexpressed anger can manifest itself in physical problems (such as headaches and indigestion) or, worse, in lashing-out behaviors. For a form of action, continue to use rewriting and action-distraction to lessen the impact of the original event. Also, consider discussing your feelings with someone who is not connected with your workplace.

As we have seen in this chapter, anger begins with intense arousal accompanied by the feeling we have been wronged. It is important to use action-distraction to keep our physiological reaction from spiraling out of control, and to minimize rumination. Once you have used rewriting to separate the problem from the emotional hook, you must decide whether or not to take action by communicating the problem. If you choose to communicate, it is important to consider what you need in order to resolve the situation. If you choose not to communicate, it is important to dissipate the pressure situation by continuing to engage in action-distraction and rewriting.

CHAPTER 11

Dealing With People Pressure

BAD INTERACTIONS with people are a key source of pressure in the workplace. People pressure often accumulates over small interactions with your immediate coworkers. This includes the team player who contributes the least, the client who is indecisive and then blames you for not getting the job done, the coworker who is going through a divorce and is quick to criticize, and the secretary who forgets to give you messages because she is on a personal call. If you look back on your week, you can probably think of more than one interaction that you wish had been handled differently.

Even if your people skills are developed, they will always be challenged by unpleasant office interactions. Indeed, research has uncovered a surprising statistic: that 20 percent of company employees encounter habitual workplace bullies. Bullies are identified as people who blame others for their errors, make unreasonable demands, criticize, inconsistently enforce arbitrary rules, make threats of job loss, use insults and put-downs, deny accomplishment, create social exclusion, yell and scream, and take credit for the work of others. Is there anyone in your workplace who seems to fit this profile?

People Pressure

This form of pressure is multiplied in business because we know that if our interpersonal skills are lacking, our careers may suffer. This is especially true for managers, who must continually interact with others. The constant interaction can feel overwhelming, with a mutual fueling between people pressure and bad interpersonal relationships. On the one hand, bad interpersonal interactions create pressure; on the other, pressure can lead to irritability, which fuels bad interpersonal interactions. Often when we are feeling irritable, we try to avoid an interaction. Unfortunately, avoidance creates more pressure by delaying the inevitable and increasing the negative beliefs that we associate with the situation.

So what can you do to alleviate people pressure? Essentially, you cannot change anyone but you, for no one else is really under your control; thus you must control your contribution to interpersonal interactions. This chapter will show you how to do that using the SBRT process. It includes suggestions for using SBRT to deal with a problematic interaction.

I. Stop

Common cues that you are under people pressure include the following: lashing out in anger, avoiding people in the work environment, mentally creating detailed scenarios of "what you would like to say" to others, ruminating, procrastinating, and having no sense of humor, a critical attitude toward others, a racing mind, and a racing heart.

2. Breathe

No matter what you are doing—whether preparing for a personal interaction or engaging in one—your immediate reaction to any of these cues should include diaphragmatic breathing. Such breathing will allow you to maintain optimal perception and energy management. When we are in a pressurized interaction, our thoughts increase in number and tend to become distorted and negative. As mentioned earlier, there is a negative physiological reaction to every negative thought. So engaging in deep breathing can mean the difference between flying off the handle and responding appropriately.

Use the Stop and Breathe steps prior to a pressure-filled interaction. If you know that a stressful interaction is coming, take 3 to 5 minutes to engage in a form of action-distraction, such as brisk mindful walking. This will clear your mind and curb any tendency to mentally rehearse the interaction—a rumination that would likely end in exaggeration, increasing stress, if you used something like the relaxation response. (For more on action-distraction, see Chapter 10.)

3. Rewrite

Often, we generate interpersonal conflict because we feel threatened, hurt, or vulnerable. This translates into negative thoughts about us or the other person. When under people pressure, we need to rewrite our automatic thoughts in and out of the interaction. Prior to the interaction, rewriting proceeds as usual; but during the interaction, rewriting takes the form of setting the thoughts aside.

Rewriting During the Interaction

Here, take the time to listen. As you breathe, look at the other person and really listen to what he or she has to say. This can be more difficult than it sounds, for it requires you to maintain a passive relationship to your thoughts—you cannot really listen if you have a running dialog in your head. If such a dialog begins, simply acknowledge that "a thought is just a thought" and refocus your attention on what the other person is saying. You will find this refocusing easier if you practice mindfulness and the relaxation response when not engaged in a pressurized situation.

Listening helps you collect the facts. Remember, the negative thoughts that accompany stressful interactions are often inaccurate. When we really listen to the other person, we gain more information with which to work. Listen, breathe, and then respond. This will help to increase the quality of the interaction.

Option for Highly Difficult Interaction

If you are trying to interact, become overwhelmed by negative thoughts, and find that the rewriting approach above is not working, then consider the option of buying time: taking a bathroom break from the interaction to collect your thoughts. A good phrase to memorize is "If you could please excuse me, can we continue this conversation in 5 minutes?" Once you have uttered this, head for the bathroom. If there is one thing that everyone acknowledges, it is that when nature calls, nature calls. Even though nature isn't calling, a bathroom stall is a good place to collect your thoughts and engage in breathing techniques and rewriting. We promise, the other person will not come in after you. If time allows, work through your thoughts, asking yourself for each one, "What is the evidence for this thought?" If there is indeed evidence for it, then ask, "Is it in my best interest to hold this thought?" Remember to look for thought distortions (see below).

Rewriting Prior to the Interaction

Prior to the interaction, examine your thoughts, trying to identify any thought distortions. Especially be on the lookout for overgeneralization ("Liam discounts everything I say"), personalization ("Maybe it *is* my fault that the four of us couldn't finish this project; so I should just take responsibility") and blame ("This whole thing is Eddie's fault because he failed to remind us of the deadline"). Two additional distortions to consider are

---

> ➤ *Self-Talk and Replacement Self-Talk: Example*

Liam discounts everything I say. What is the evidence for this? Liam did not use my idea on this project and did not respond to my email inquiry about the project. He did use my idea last year on the Smith account. For reasons that I have no knowledge of, Liam chose to go with Jen's idea instead of mine this time. I also have no information as to why he did not respond to my email. I am disappointed that my idea was not used, but this does not necessarily mean that my ideas will be overlooked in the future.

I bet he thinks Bill did a better job. What is the evidence for this? Bill and I turned in reports on the Paris account. I know there was marketing information that I chose not to include. At the same time, I have no knowledge of what was included in Bill's report. Nor do I have any knowledge of whether the Boss was interested in that marketing sector—that's why I left it out in the first place.

"mind-reading" ("I bet he thinks Bill did a better job") and "fortune-telling" ("If I say this, Ken will fly off the handle").

Challenge the thoughts. In particular, challenge the threat. Perceiving a situation as threatening may be irrational or distorted. Finally, engage in self-talk and replacement self-talk.

4. Take Action

Here this step involves interaction. As usual, before taking action, make sure you have separated the emotional hook from the problem to be solved. Also be sure to do the following:

- Recognize what you need from the interaction.
- Make an attempt to empathize.
- Identify your possible approaches.

When time is short, it becomes difficult (if not impossible) to engage in all these preliminaries. However, if you practice these considerations when time is available, you will become adept enough at them to apply them on the spot.

Separate the Emotional Hook From the Problem

When you are dealing with people pressure, separating the emotional hook from the problem can take some extra effort. This is because we may have negative feelings left over from past interactions or feelings that may have arisen as a product of thought distortions.

For example, Mark was Kerri's manager. He tended to bark orders at her and yell when things were not done correctly. Mark told Kerri to design promotional materials for a special account. Kerri immediately felt pressured because she had never designed promotional material before and did not fully understand what it entailed. She doubted her ability to do the task and figured that Mark would explode if she created something inappropriate. Her initial instinct was to avoid Mark because she didn't want to look stupid.

Kerri did not act on that instinct, however, because she was familiar with the SBRT process. After taking a few deep breaths, she tuned in to her thoughts to separate the emotional hook from the problem. Primarily she was engaging in fortune-telling and emotional reasoning. Because Mark's yelling had left her feeling inadequate in the past, she assumed she would look stupid and not be able to perform the job adequately this time.

Through rewriting, Kerri realized that she did not know if she had the skills to complete this project because she had never tried one like it. She also realized that she had completed new projects before, so there was no reason to think she could not tackle this one if she had more information. The problem to be solved was a lack of information on what promotional materials consisted of.

Recognize What You Need From the Interaction

Once you have identified the problem, the next step is to clarify whether or not you can get what you need from further interaction with the other person. The best way to clarify your needs is to write them down, being as specific and concrete as possible. If you are thinking "I can skip that part," you are mistaken. Write your needs down. It is not enough to think about them. The mind has a way of hanging on to thought distortions and, if left to its own devices, will again confuse the problem with the emotional hook.

For example, Kerri may decide that she only needs support to start this new project. Because she can acquire the information herself, there is no reason to engage Mark in further interaction; she can obtain the support from someone with whom she feels more comfortable. However, it is also possible for Kerri to decide that she needs to see an example of promotional materials from a previous account. In this case, she now has a specific request to give Mark or anyone else who has access to this material. Finally, Kerri may decide that she needs to ask Mark for specifics on what he is looking for.

Once you know what you need to get from the interaction, be clear and specific about asking for it. This is the fastest way to get your needs met and avoid conflict in an interaction. If you do not speak up, it is unlikely that you will get what you need. Reflect on a time when you wished someone would provide you with information and you did not receive it; quite likely, you did not speak up. Ask (specifically and clearly), and you shall receive.

Make an Attempt to Empathize

One way to avoid stressful interactions is to empathize with others, imagining how they are feeling in the situation. Before the interaction, carefully consider how your approach will make the other person feel and how he or she is likely to react. (In doing this, be careful not to create thought distortions.) If you predict conflict or hostility, recognize that this conflict or hostility may have nothing to do with you. Ask yourself, "Why might this person react this way?"

One way to answer that question is to imagine yourself as the other person and provide the answer in the person's "own" words. This exercise can help you feel where the other person is coming from and give you valuable information regarding what you can and cannot contribute to the interaction.

Identify Your Possible Approaches

Next, identify possible approaches to the interaction. Sometimes distance is helpful. If you do not feel confident engaging in a face-to-face interaction, try calling the person on the phone or sending an email.

Phoning is similar to a face-to-face interaction. If you choose this option, make sure you do the following before dialing:

- Write down what you need from the interaction. Do not rely on your memory for this, or you may end up with thought distortions.

- Engage in deep breathing. This will calm you and help you focus your thoughts.

Email has special, beneficial properties for helping us deal with people pressure:

- First, we must write out our thoughts. It is then clear whether or not we are (a) stating what we need in specific terms, and (b) engaging in thought distortions.

- Second, email is not necessarily an immediate form of communication.

When you are under people pressure, do not send email immediately. Let at least 5 minutes pass between writing the email and reviewing it. When reviewing, assess each sentence by asking, "Is this pertinent to the situation at hand?" and "Is this exactly what I mean?" If it is not exactly what you mean, change it. If you read a sentence and it seems to have an emotional undertone, take it out and separate the emotion in one sentence and the point in another sentence. Before sending, decide whether or not the emotional sentence is necessary or helpful to the situation.

Whatever approach you use, ask yourself what is more important: winning (in the interaction) or solving the problem? Even when you think you are right, simply winning the argument will not solve the problem. The interaction will be optimal if both parties get what they need from the interaction. Remember, you will likely have to deal with this person again in the future.

Taking Action: Communication and Interaction

Now you are ready to begin the communication and interact. Keep in mind that mood matters. While interacting, make an attempt to maintain a positive outlook. Instead of taking the typical approach of fortune-telling and predicting a negative outcome, try to assume that the course of the interaction is unknowable. In reality, there are an infinite number of outcomes to any interaction. We all like to work with people who have a positive attitude; therefore, approaching a problem situation in a positive way can make the difference between a productive interaction and a destructive one.

As we have seen in this chapter, dealing with people pressure can make or break your career. Because the only person you can really control is you, the way to work with people pressure is to control your contribution to the interaction. By carefully rewriting any misperceptions and inaccuracies, you can acknowledge any problem that needs to be solved and then attempt to solve it. Remember to utilize deep breathing in and out of the interaction. Prior to the interaction, separate the problem from the emotional hook, delineate what you need from the interaction, try to empathize, and consider your approach options. During the interaction try to maintain a positive attitude, take the time to listen, and be aware that you can postpone the interaction if need be.

CHAPTER 12

Dealing With Fatigue Pressure

ALL OF US have periods of fatigue. For some of us, though, fatigue is chronic. According to a poll by the National Sleep Foundation, 65 percent of us do not get enough sleep. The pressure of fatigue comes from the need to be productive despite the fact that we are tired. There are many obstacles in this attempt at productivity. Tiredness makes us emotional (impatient, anxious, depressed), makes it difficult to think clearly, creates muscular tension, and hampers motivation. These factors are estimated to cost businesses 18 billion dollars a year.

Fatigue is insidious because it interacts with on-the-job pressure. Most of us know that job pressure can create anxiety and that anxiety can interfere with a person's ability to sleep. Job pressure thus can lead to sleep deprivation and fatigue. What many people do not realize is that a lack of sleep increases muscular tightness and anxiety. In other words, sleep deprivation increases tension. Although we may not be conscious of it, we use tension as a coping mechanism to maintain alertness. So job pressure and fatigue feed off each other.

Fatigue Pressure

There are two different fatigue syndromes: task specific and generalized.

- **Task-specific fatigue.** If someone has been engaged in a task for a long period of time, task-specific fatigue and boredom can occur. This will manifest itself as work slowdown and distraction.

- **Generalized fatigue.** This is caused by sleep deprivation, exhaustion, or burn-out. The major symptoms are emotionalism and lack of motivation. In this state, people become unwilling to exert control over or put effort into performance. They tend to opt for easier work strategies even if these strategies are not optimal. The problem is exacerbated by their further unwillingness to put any effort into coping strategies.

One should deal with both types of fatigue pressure by practicing the SBRT method.

I. Stop

Obviously, the major cues for fatigue are tiredness and a lack of energy. Other cues include lack of motivation, poor concentration, procrastination, indecisiveness, emotionalism, forgetfulness, confusion, hopelessness, meaninglessness, pessimism, insomnia, tight muscles, and a general inability to get things done.

2. Breathe

The goal of this step is to eliminate unnecessary tension and maintain alertness through mindful movement. There are two forms of alertness: tense alertness and relaxed alertness. You want to strive for the latter because the former is just a waste of energy—the very resource that, being tired, you do not have enough of.

When you notice fatigue cues, begin to engage in deep breathing. Such breathing, in and of itself, will raise your level of alertness. Next, engage in mindful progressive relaxation or mindful movement. The breathing and movement will eliminate unnecessary tension and the mindfulness component will help you reach a state of relaxed alertness.

Some people find that this step alone will wake them up and help them return to increased productivity. Particularly if your fatigue is task-specific, engaging in the Stop and Breathe steps may be enough to help alleviate the problem.

3. Rewrite

None of the SBRT steps are easy when you are tired. Rewriting is particularly difficult. When you are fatigued, your thought process will revert to habit. This is because habits require the least amount of effort. If you are a person whose thoughts habitually become distorted (by now you know who you are), then you will have a preponderance of favorite distortions to deal with. Remember: These distorted thoughts are not true; they are just easy for you to think.

Whether your automatic thoughts habitually become distorted or not, watch out for statements containing the words *should, must,* and *have to.* When we are tired, we usually feel the pressure to "have to" perform and get things done.

Challenge your thoughts. Since these thoughts are habitual, be particularly sensitive to the question "What is the evidence for this?" Also, habits put us into a very narrow frame of mind, so it is good to ask, "Is there another way of seeing the situation?" and "Is it in my best interest to hold this belief?" Engage in self-talk—and talk back with positives and accurate answers.

4. Take Action

Your first response to tiredness should be task switching in order to assess whether or not the tiredness is task-specific or generalized. If your fatigue is task-specific, switching tasks is the best remedy. If switching tasks does not help, your fatigue may be generalized.

In task switching, it is good to remember that the more different the second task is from the first, the more effective the switch will be in relieving fatigue pressure. Of course, switching to a task that is more interesting will always help too. For example, switching from editing one document to editing another will not be of much help in alleviating task-specific fatigue; on the other hand, switching from editing a document to brainstorming with a colleague about a future project will do the trick.

If you discover you're dealing with a case of generalized fatigue, the best remedy is rest or sleep.

Napping as an Intervention

If sleep deprivation is restricted to a single night, napping can be a useful intervention. A 30-minute nap can alleviate the effects of fatigue. If you have the time, napping for up to an hour has been shown to increase performance. Napping, however, is not necessarily helpful for generalized fatigue. This is primarily because you will (a) sleep for too long or (b) wake up groggy because your body needs to sleep for a longer period of time.

If it is practical to take a nap, do so, but be careful not to ruminate. It is useless to lie down for 30 minutes and think about all the things that need to be done. Instead, use mindfulness to put you to sleep. Specifically:

- Count down your exhales from 100 to 1.
- If your mind wanders, return your attention to your breathing.

Since the goal is a nap, at best you will fall asleep. At worst, you will have engaged in an excellent relaxation exercise and decreased wasted energy.

What Not to Do

Whether your fatigue is task-specific or generalized, try not to reach for coffee as a quick fix. Many of us do this in an attempt to energize. Although caffeine is a stimulant, it also contributes to dehydration. The major symptom of dehydration is tiredness!

Making a To-Do List

You also can lessen the impact of fatigue by completing tasks in a certain order. If possible, do complex, important tasks first thing in the morning, for fatigue increases as the day progresses. Your clarity and productivity will be at its peak in the morning.

The best approach is to make a to-do list when you first get to work. In the case of fatigue, there are four steps:

1. List everything that must be completed today.

2. Go through the list and divide it into what you must do, should do, and want to do.

3. Review the "must" and "should" options. In reviewing, (a) reassess to see if you can eliminate a few things, and (b) consider delegating the task to someone else. Remember, you are not the only employee. Other company members can contribute to the task.

4. Order the tasks in terms of complexity. You will want to start your work with the most complex task or the task that requires the most complex thought.

As you work through the tasks on your list, focus solely on whatever task you are completing. Multi-tasking will just make you more tired.

Also, whenever you feel fatigue symptoms creeping in, take a break. This is an immediate switching of tasks, even if the new task only requires getting a drink of water. If the break does not help relieve your fatigue, switch to a different task on the list. The new task must be less complex (that is, further down on the list).

If you hit a point where you feel that all of the tasks are too complex, break them into subtasks. Every piece of work that you do can be broken down into subtasks. Once you have done this, select a subtask and try to complete it. Although efficiency experts suggest finishing every task that you begin (because revisiting the same task is too time-consuming), you must weigh efficiency and quality. Completing a complex task while under extreme fatigue will not lead to the highest-quality work.

Dealing With Generalized Fatigue

Although the SBRT technique will help alleviate the pressure of generalized fatigue, daily management of chronic fatigue will not make the problem go away. On your own time, you need to assess the reasons for chronic fatigue. They could be any of a wide variety of things. Common causes are extreme pressure, insomnia, lack of exercise, a bad diet (e.g., one with too much sugar and caffeine), excessive alcohol or drug consumption, or depression. Each of these causes may be contributing to or exacerbated by insomnia or difficulty falling asleep. (Note that using SBRT before going to bed can help remedy insomnia.) Be aware that some of these issues may require professional intervention.

As we have seen in this chapter, fatigue pressure is widespread, insidious, and difficult to tackle. Whether you are experiencing task-specific fatigue or generalized fatigue, you cannot function effectively under this stressor. Task-specific pressure can be dealt with and alleviated by using SBRT, particularly the strategy of task switching. However, generalized fatigue must be dealt with through rest or sleep. Be honest with yourself if you suffer from generalized fatigue, and address the personal issues that may be causing it.

CHAPTER 13

Dealing With Evaluation Pressure

EVALUATION PRESSURE typically manifests itself as worry. You might worry about the quality of your work, your personal interactions in the office, or your most recent presentation or report. Worry creates a negative focus. It puts you in the mindset of looking for problems. It makes decision-making difficult, decreases efficiency, and makes you feel generally overwhelmed.

Worry does serve a purpose, though. It alerts you to problems, prepares you for action, and helps you develop coping mechanisms through "rehearsal" of the worrisome event. Worry is most useful when it leads to a successful approach for coping with pressure. At all other times, it is pointless and a waste of energy.

Evaluation Pressure

Here the goal of engaging in the SBRT process is to use the energy associated with worry to create a successful approach to the problem at hand. At the same time, we also want to use the SBRT process to maintain an orientation to the present that will help offset the worry.

I. Stop

Worry puts you into a planning mode; therefore, the most typical cues for worry include rumination, obsessive planning, concentration problems, predicting the worst, a racing mind, fear, a racing heart, insomnia, nervous habits, and restlessness.

2. Breathe

When we are going to be evaluated, we tend to obsess about either one of two things:

- What will happen in the future
- What has happened in the past

This step's major goal is thus to stay in the present; you want to focus your attention on things that are happening now and put the past and future aside. Luckily this "present orientation" is the goal of every mindfulness technique; therefore, any mindfulness technique is appropriate when you are under evaluation pressure.

The Use of Categorization

In practicing mindfulness for evaluation pressure, you also want to use a categorization technique that will help you maintain your present orientation. Any mindfulness practice requires focusing your attention on present sensations and trying to maintain a passive disregard for

---

> ➤ *Mindfulness Technique With Categorization:*
> *Example*
>
> The following is a description of what may occur in your mind
> during the practice of a mindfulness technique with categorization.
> Notice the labels "memory" and "fantasy."
>
> *Feeling the in-breath as it comes through my nose; feeling the out-*
> *breath as my chest falls; "My boss is going to hate my presentation*
> *—Fantasy"; "The last presentation was nerve-wracking—Memory";*
> *attention on breathing; feeling the in-breath as it comes through my*
> *nose; feeling the out-breath as my stomach deflates; "It's so difficult*
> *to print out slides from my computer—Memory"; "What if I run out*
> *of picture-quality paper?—Fantasy" [and so on].*

any extraneous thoughts that arise. Here, this passive
disregard will be difficult because your thoughts are
likely to include plans to help you deal with the evaluation (this is jumping ahead to the Take Action step).

To counter the effect of these thoughts, put each arising
thought into either one of two categories:

- Memory—thoughts about the past
- Fantasy—thoughts about the future

Then discard the thought.

Remember, the point of this second step is to establish
and maintain a present orientation. Any thought that
draws your attention to the past or the future thus should
be categorized and then discarded.

3. Rewrite

Worry tends to create a self-focus. When you are under this type of pressure, be especially careful not to use the rewriting step to criticize yourself. The goal is to assess the accuracy of your thoughts. Do not distort the evidence. If you hold a negative belief about yourself, ask, "Is it in my best interest to hold this belief?"

As usual, notice automatic thoughts. Words to watch out for are *must, have to,* and *ought.* You will probably find yourself thinking of things you "ought" to do or "ought" to have done for the evaluation. Just as with anger pressure, you may find you are "making plans" and fueling the chain of thoughts. Be careful that you are not contributing to inaccuracies or distortions.

Be sure to identify distortions. Evaluation pressure tends to prompt all-or-nothing thinking, overgeneralization, mental filter, discounting the positive, and fortune-telling. Remember, anything you think might happen during the evaluation is fortune-telling.

Finally, challenge your thoughts. As with other types of pressure, the following are good questions to use: *What is the evidence for this? Is there another way of seeing this? Is it in my best interest to hold this belief?* After assessing the accuracy of the thoughts, also ask these questions: *What is the worst that could happen? Is this under my control?* Often evaluation worry is exacerbated by the thought that the outcome will be extreme. If you actually identify "the worst that could happen," you will likely see that, in most cases, you have the resources to handle the worst possible scenario. Engage in self-talk, and talk back with positives and accurate answers.

4. Take Action

Identify the possible solutions. As in the case of anger, there are times to act and times to "let it go" (by engaging in breathing and rewriting). The decision of whether or not to take action is made by answering the question "Is this under my control?" When something is out of our control, worrying becomes a waste of energy and distracts from the things we can control.

For example, Barbara's annual report was sent to the national office this afternoon. Company representatives took it home with them this evening and will be reviewing the report in a meeting first thing tomorrow morning. If Barbara is worried that a particular figure is unclear, she can take action and fax a new figure to the national office before the meeting; thus she can control the situation. On the other hand, if she is worried about the content of an entire section of the report, the situation may now be beyond her control. This would be the time to "let it go." The report is already in, and this would be a bad idea to change it, even if she created the time to do so. Her time is better spent focusing on the present and turning her attention to another project.

If the Situation Is Under Your Control

If you feel that you can take sufficient control of the situation and choose to act, follow these steps:

1. Reevaluate the necessity of taking action by asking, "How important is the thing I'm worrying about? How much energy is worth expending on this worry?" This question will help you eliminate the unimportant. For example, in answering this question, Barbara may realize that the figure is clearly explained in the text and revising it is not worth company time.

2. If you still decide to take action, try to take action immediately. To speed the process, make a list of possible solutions to the problem and then list the pros and cons of each solution. Next, take some action, even if it is small. Writing out a plan and initiating that plan will help alleviate worry.

If you find it is impossible to take immediate action, then use writing, distraction, and mindfulness to keep you in the present. For example, we often find ourselves vulnerable to worry before we go to bed at night, in which case we cannot take action immediately. To deal with this problem (and ward off insomnia), try this technique:

1. Write down what you are worrying about and how you can take action. This will provide you with a plan and leave no reason to obsess about the topic of worry.

2. Distract yourself with something unrelated to the topic of worry, such as reading a chapter in a book.

3. Use deep breathing and mindfulness techniques right before getting into bed.

If the Situation Is Not Under Your Control

"Let go" when the worry is not under your control, and use writing, distraction, and mindfulness to keep you in the present. Try the following:

1. Write down what you are worrying about. Also, record your answers to the questions that helped you decide the situation is beyond your control. This will reinforce the fact that the worry is a waste of energy.

2. Distract yourself with something unrelated to the topic of worry; in addition, use deep breathing and mindfulness techniques to keep you in the present.

Keep in mind that your imagination can serve as a distraction to offset the worry. Simply imagine a positive, happy outcome for the stressful situation. Your body does not know the difference between what you are imagining and what is real; so instead of worrying about a negative outcome, specifically imagine a positive outcome.

As we have seen in this chapter, evaluation creates worry. Worry can be useful if it helps you create a plan for action; otherwise, it is a waste of energy. You can use the SBRT technique to maintain a focus on the present, to decide whether to act on the source of the worry, and to help you "let it go" if the situation is beyond your control.

In Conclusion . . .

IN THIS ERA OF UNCERTAINTY, it seems that everyone in today's workplace is under more pressure. Study after study shows that managing stress is a growing challenge. People usually think of stress as something entirely negative, but as we have seen, stress has tangible benefits when managed properly.

Again, the critical task for managers is to gain a better understanding of stress in the workplace, in their organizations, and in their teams and employees. Anyone in a position of organizational or team leadership should be tracking the issue of stress. In general, good management practices will likely reduce unhealthy stress by improving employee autonomy, training, working conditions, schedules, career development, support systems, communication, relationships with supervisors, and reward opportunities. However, the most direct action a manager can take to reduce unhealthy stress is to identify and remove unnecessary stressors from the workplace. Stress-management best practices should also be considered.

When a person over whom you have direct supervisory authority in the workplace is suffering the effects of poorly managed stress, you must take action to help. Depending upon the nature and gravity of the situation, you may or may not be the one to provide the ultimate solution. Yet, as the employee's manager, it is your responsibility to engage the person appropriately and effectively, to evaluate the problem, and to provide access to support or take direct action to help alleviate the person's stress. Of course, there are considerable limits to what a manager can do to help employees manage stress in the workplace. Ultimately, to perform under pressure, employees must develop stress management skills.

Helping individuals learn to manage stress and work well under pressure has been the principle focus of this pocket guide. We strongly urge leaders and managers to provide employees with resources and training in the Stop, Breathe, Rewrite, and Take Action approach. SBRT will help them develop stress management skills and learn to perform more effectively under pressure. It is our great hope that the material in this pocket guide will help you provide such resources and training.

References and Further Resources

American Institute for Cognitive Therapy, NY, New York.

American Psychiatric Association, Washington, DC.

American Psychological Association, Washington, DC.

American Psychological Society, Washington, DC.

Association for the Advancement of Behavior Therapy, NY, New York.

Atkinson, W. (2000). Strategies for Workplace Stress. *Risk & Insurance,* 11(13).

Benson, H. (1975). *The Relaxation Response.* NY: William Morrow.

Benson, H., & Stuart, E. M. (1992). *The Wellness Book: The Comprehensive Guide to Maintaining Health and Treating Stress-Related Illness.* NY: Simon & Schuster.

Berk, L. S., Tan, S. A., Fry, W. F., Napier, B. J., Lee, J. W., Hubbard, R. W., Lewis, J. E., & Eby, W. C. (1989). Neuroendocrine and Stress Hormone Changes During Mirthful Laughter. *American Journal of the Medical Sciences,* 298, 390–96.

Bloomfield H. H., & Cooper, R. K. (1995). *The Power of 5.* Emmaus, Pennsylvania: Rodale Press.

Burns, D. D. (1989). *The Feeling Good Handbook: Using the New Mood Therapy in Everyday Life.* NY: William Morrow.

Butler, G., & Hope, T. (1995). *Managing Your Mind: The Mental Fitness Guide.* NY: Oxford University Press.

Cooper, C. L. (1985). The Road to Health in American Firms. *New Society.* 335–336.

Craig, A., & Cooper, R. E. (1992). Symptoms of Acute and Chronic Fatigue. In A. P. Smith & D. M. Jones (Eds.), *Handbook of Human Performance, Volume 3: Trait and State.* London, Academic Press.

Danna, K., & Griffin, R. W. (1999). Health and Well-being in the Workplace: A Review and Synthesis of the Literature. *Journal of Management,* 25(3).

DeCarlo, D. T. (2001). More on Workplace Stress. *Risk & Insurance,* 12(13).

Desmond, P. A., & Matthews, G. (1997). Implications of Task-Induced Fatigue Effects for In-Vehicle Counter-measures to Driver Fatigue. *Accident Analysis and Prevention,* 29, 513–523.

Elkin, A. J., & Rosch, P. J. (1990). Promoting Mental Health at the Workplace: The Prevention Side of Stress Management. *Occupational Medicine: State of the Art Review,* 5, 739–754.

Ellis, A., & Greiger, R. (1977). *Handbook of Rational Emotive Therapy.* NY: Springer.

Gaskill, M. (2001). Bullies Bring Trouble From the Schoolyard to the Workplace. *Business First— Columbus,* 18(18).

Gibson, D., & Tulgan, B. (2001). *Managing Anger in the Workplace.* Amherst, MA: HRD Press.

GrandJean, E. (1991). *Fitting the Task to the Man* (3rd ed.). NY: Taylor.

Hockey, G. R. J. (1997). Compensatory Control in the Regulation of Human Performance Under Stress and High Workload: A Cognitive-Energetical Framework. *Biological Psychology,* 45, 73–93.

Holding, D. H. (1983). Fatigue. In G. R. J. Hockey (Ed.), *Stress and Fatigue in Human Performance.* Chichester: John Wiley & Sons Ltd.

Johnson, P. R., & Indvik, J. (1997). The Boomer Blues: Depression in the Workplace. *Public Personnel Management,* 26: 359–365.

Karasek, R. A., & Theorell, T. (1990). *Healthy Work, Stress, Productivity, and the Reconstruction of Working Life.* NY: Basic Books.

Kohn, P. M. (1996). On Coping Adaptively With Daily Hassles. In M. Zeider & N. S. Endler (Eds.), *Handbook of Coping: Theory, Research, Application.* NY: John Wiley & Sons Inc.

Krivyanski, M. (2001). Stress Busters. *The Business Journal—Milwaukee,* 18(41).

Lazarus, R. S., & Folkman, S. (1984). *Stress, Appraisal, and Coping.* NY: Springer.

Maier, S. F., & Watkins, L. R. (2000). The Immune System as a Sensory System: Implications for Psychology. *Current Directions in Psychological Science,* 9(3), 98–102.

Maslach, C., & Jackson, S. E. (1981). The Measurement of Experienced Burnout. *Journal of Occupational Behavior,* 2, 99–113.

Matthews, G., Jones, D. M., & Chamberlain, A. G. (1990). Refining the Measurement of Mood: The UWIST Mood Adjective Checklist. *British Journal of Psychology,* 81, 17–42.

Matthews, G., Joyner, L., Gilliland, K., Campbell, S. E., Huggins, J., & Falconer, S. (1999). Validation of a Comprehensive Stress State Questionnaire: Towards a State "Big Three?" In I. Mervielde, I. J. Deary, F. De Fruyt, & F. Ostendorf (Eds.), *Personality Psychology in Europe* (Vol. 7). Tilburg: Tilburg University Press.

National Association of Social Workers, Washington, DC.

National Institute of Mental Health, Bethesda, Maryland.

National Mental Health Association, Alexandria, Virginia.

National Sleep Foundation (2002). Sleep Strategies for Shift Workers. Retrieved June 2002 from www.sleepfoundation.org.

Neuman, J. H., & Baron, R. A. (1997). Aggression in the Workplace. In R. A. Giacalone & J. Greenberg (Eds.), *Antisocial Behavior in Organizations* (pp. 37–67). Thousand Oaks, CA: Sage Publications.

O'Leary-Kelly, A., Griffin, R. W., & Glew, D. J. (1996). Organization-Motivated Aggression: A Research Framework. *The Academy of Management Review,* 21, 225–253.

Simmons, K. (2001). Warning! Bullies at Work, Career Builder. *The Business Journal—Milwaukee,* 18(41), 2.

Sparks, K., Cooper, C. L., Fried, Y., & Shirom, A. (1997). The Effect of Hours of Work on Health: A Meta-Analytic Review. *Journal of Occupational and Organizational Psychology,* 70(4), 391–409.

Thayer, R. E. (1978). Factor Analytic and Reliability Studies on the Activation-Deactivation Adjective Checklist. *Psychological Reports,* 42, 747–756.

Tulgan, B. (2001). *Winning the Talent Wars.* NY: W.W. Norton.

Turkington, C. A. (1998). *Stress Management for Busy People.* NY: McGraw-Hill.

Vaillant, G. E. (1977). *Adaptation to Life.* Boston: Little, Brown.

Van Velsor, E. V., & Leslie, J. B. (1995). Why Executives Derail: Perspectives Across Time and Cultures. *The Academy of Management Executive,* 9, 62–72.

Wells, A., & Matthews, G. (1994). *Attention and Emotion: A Clinical Perspective.* Hove, UK: Lawrence Erlbaum Associates Ltd.

Appendix
List of Employee Support Services

Corporate Wellness Programs

- Athletic facilities and fitness programs such as aerobics and stretching/toning, basketball, volleyball, in-line skating, golf, soccer, softball, and rock climbing
- Personal wellness budgets for employees to spend at will
- Massage therapy
- Dedicated time and resources for napping, including nap rooms with mattresses or couches, washable sleeping bags, pillows, blankets, alarm clocks, eyeshades, and cassette-tape headphone sets
- Full-service onsite health clinics
- Onsite healthcare services, including testing, screenings, and assessments of employees' particular health risks; nurses to discuss test results; and literature on common disorders and health needs
- Civic involvement and personal wellness through community wellness: paid leave for the time contributed to employee-chosen nonprofit organizations in community, including hours during regular work hours

Family Care

- Toll-free telephone consultation and referral services
- Eldercare ranging from advice to facilities offering roundtrip transportation, meals, nursing care, exercise classes, and assistance with daily routines like showering and grooming
- Childcare including onsite centers, childcare spending accounts, back-up childcare, and school-holiday and after-school programs
- Prenatal care and lactation programs
- Onsite schooling
- Pet care

Corporate Concierge Services

Personal Services:

- Personal Shopping
- Moving Services
- Decorating Services
- Landscaping Services
- Home Repair
- Courier Service
- Dry-Cleaning/Laundry
- Car Wash/AirCare
- Automotive Repairs
- Party Staffing

Travel Arrangements:

- Hotel Reservations
- Private Home/Condo Rentals
- Airline Reservations
- Visa/Passport Assistance
- Ground Transportation
- Translation Services
- Golf, Ski, Adventure Packages
- Personal Document Library

Meeting Planning:
- Site Selection
- Conference Registration
- Conference Materials
- Professional Speakers
- Entertainment
- Wine Tastings
- VIP Arrangements
- Off-Site Dining
- Onsite Catering
- Audiovisual Services
- Incentive Trips
- Public Relations

Professional Services:
- Audiovisual Equipment
- Cellular Phone Rentals
- Language Translation
- Computer Training/ Seminars
- Computer Rental/ Purchase/Repair
- Corporate Motivational Programs
- Courier Services
- Placement Services
- Complete Office Relocation Services
- Complete Small Business Programs
- Trade Show Marketing
- Meeting Materials
- Website Design/ Marketing
- Chauffer Services
- Focus Groups
- Photography
- Videography
- Printing and Reprographics
- Temporary Staffing Services
- Public Relations
- Business Associates

Entertainment Services:
- Concert, Theatre, Sports Tickets
- Private Club Arrangements
- Restaurant Reservations
- Tee Times and Tennis Court Bookings
- Fitness Trainers
- Massage Services
- Catering Services
- Musicians, Bands, Orchestras

Visitor Management:

- Airport Meet and Greets
- Transfers
- Accommodation Arrangements
- City Tours
- Dining Arrangements
- Visitor Gifts
- Area Maps/Information
- Complete Relocation Services

Miscellaneous:

- Babysitters and Nannies
- Balloons and Gift Baskets
- Vancouver After Dark
- Dinner Theatres
- Film Developing
- Airport Pickup/Drop Off
- Emergency Pickup
- Floral Arrangements and Delivery
- Grocery Delivery
- Haircuts
- Kennels and Veterinary Services
- Locksmiths
- Shoe Shine and Repair
- Tailoring and Alterations
- Wedding Planning
- Liquor Delivery